Yugoslavia

Crisis and Disintegration

Branko Mikasinovich

"Yugoslavia-Crises and Disintegration" received the American Association of Slavic Studies prestigious "Misha Djordjevic Award" as 1995 Book of the Year

"It is excellent and objective presentation of events unfolding during the crisis and civil war in the former Yugoslavia."
Belgrade news magazine NIN

PREFACE

Hardly ever in the past, has the mass media, as the most influential instrument in the era of information, played such a crucial and biased role as it has in the Yugoslav conflict. The mass media succeeded in creating stereotypes about Serbs, Croats, and Moslems, and the overall Yugoslav situation, which was largely defined without regard for history, social or political structure, reality, ongoing changes, or ultimately the truth. This book provides a concise and objective background on Yugoslavia and the events leading to the Yugoslav crisis and the civil war.

The author would like to thank his spouse, Mrs. Nellie Mikasinovich for her valuable suggestions.

CONTENTS

FROM A KINGDOM TO TITOISM

A BRIEF HISTORICAL BACKGROUND

Communist Yugoslavia was often described as a country with six republics, five nationalities, three languages, three religions and two alphabets. The six republics were Serbia, Montenegro, Croatia, Slovenia, Bosnia-Herzegovina and Macedonia; the languages were Serbo-Croatian, Slovenian and Macedonian; the religions Eastern Orthodoxy, Catholicism, and Islam; and two alphabets Cyrillic and Latin. After the country disintegrated, so did the Serbo-Croatian language, which became known as Serbian by the Serbs and Croatian by the Croats.

The Balkan peninsula has always been considered the crossroads between Europe and Asia. At the beginning of the Christian Era, the Roman Empire united the eastern and western regions of the Mediterranean. Upon the fall of Rome, the empire gradually split into eastern and western domains. Later, when Christianity divided into Roman Catholicism and Eastern Orthodoxy, the line was drawn through the middle of what would become Yugoslavia.

Chronic tensions were inspired by religious divisions amplified by historical developments. The Slovenes and most of the Croats were for centuries a part of the Austrian Empire and are Roman Catholics. Montenegrins, Macedonians, and Serbs are Eastern (Serbian) Orthodox. Macedonians, most of the Serbs and some Montenegrins were subjected to four hundred years of Turkish domination. Bosnian Moslems, although Slavic in race and language, practice Islam. Despite clear religious differences from the outset, all nationalities and confessions hoped to find in

1

the newly created state of Yugoslavia a source of unity, not division.

The main task facing the Yugoslav state created in 1918 -- originally called the Kingdom of the Serbs, Croats and Slovenes -- was that of integration and unification, a kind of Yugoslav *et pluribus unum*. In 1919, on the eve of the first general elections, over forty political parties were active, representing a cross-section of Yugoslavia's national, religious, ideological, and social elements. In the countryside, agrarian reform produced satisfactory results. The election results showed a vote split mainly along national and religious lines among several major parties, while declining economic conditions in the cities provided fertile ground for Communist propaganda and activity.

Compounding the growing domestic problems was the conflict between two views conditioned by historical experience. Serbia went into the union as a monarchy with its own dynasty, a sovereign and independent state recognized as such by the European Great Powers at the Congress of Berlin in 1878. Being small, it had developed a unitary system as there was no need for anything different. The Serbs went into the union because it gave all Serbs a long-sought opportunity to live together in the same state. At that time, Serbs were in the majority in Bosnia-Herzegovina and the Serbs considered it theirs and unjustly kept away from them by the Great Powers. They wanted Bosnia-Herzegovina and access to the Adriatic Sea. Being on the victorious side at the end of World War I, the Serbs were offered all of that and more. They declined the offer, however, not wanting to start the new union on a negative note and be resented by the Croatians.

The Croats, on the other hand, had no state of their own since the eleventh century, when the crown was taken over by Hungary following a convincing military victory that destroyed the Croatian armies in 1096 at Petrovo Brdo. They joined the Serbs and the Slovenes, seeking security and hoping to quickly take over the leadership of the new country. The evolving conflict between Serbian centralism and the Croatian search for self-rule served only to broaden the gap between two largest Yugoslav peoples. Intensified political conflicts led to bloody civil strife between Serbs and Croats in World War II and massive genocide of the Serbs in the Nazi-established "Independent State of Croatia." Ultimately, as one of many consequences of the success of the Communist movement, ethnic and other social divisions were effectively suppressed until well after the death of Yugoslavia's long-time dictator, Josip Broz Tito. The key to Tito's ability to hold together the various and divergent Yugoslav nationalities was his political maneuvering and liberal application of force.

THE YUGOSLAV KINGDOM

Yugoslavia was created from two existing independent Serbian kingdoms, Serbia and Montenegro, plus newly freed regions of the former Austro-Hungarian empire. These included most of the present-day Slovenia, Croatia, Dalmatia, Slavonia, Bosnia-Herzegovina, and Vojvodina. Of these, many were Serb majority regions considered to be distinct geographical entities. To foster national integration by creating a supra-nationality, the name of the Kingdom of the Serbs, Croats and Slovenes was changed to the Kingdom of Yugoslavia in 1929, and a new Yugoslav nationality was legally born. Inasmuch as the new state under the scepter of King Alexander Karadjordjevic was a child of president Woodrow Wilson's Fourteen Points, the United States was the leading force for obtaining its international recognition.

The Yugoslav idea originated in the 19th century among South Slavic intellectuals with the goal of uniting their peoples into a common state. But the road toward unification was full of contradictions. The problem was that the parties interested in joining together in one state did so for different and, as it turned out, incompatible reasons. Croats and Slovenes approached the union with Serbia zealously, since Serbia already had a sovereign kingdom, state structure, and institutions. In addition

3

to emotional reasons, Croats and Slovenes saw the creation of a new kingdom as a guarantee for their future security, and a way to evade defeat at the end of World War I, while preserving their territorial and national integrity.

In order to break down national divisions, King Alexander, reorganized Yugoslavia administratively by creating nine provinces. The centralized governmental framework, preferred by Serbs, created the perception among them that Yugoslavia was in the final stage of liberation and unification of all Serbs in one common state, their age-old dream. On the other hand, the Croats, who enjoyed limited autonomy under Austro-Hungarian rule, wanted a federation that would secure their national identity in the new kingdom, using Yugoslavia as a transitory entity. As hard as it may be to believe, the Croatian leadership expressed a desire to secede only four months after the agreement on unification was signed. Accordingly, two different structural concepts, based on two different historical and political experiences, became the new state's most difficult challenge, which eventually led to similar demands by other national groups.

The leading Yugoslav parties of the 1920s and 1930s were the Serbian Democratic Party, the Serbian Radical Party, the Croatian Peasant Party and the Slovenian Clerical People's Party. The Serbian Radical Party, headed by Nikola Pasic, attracted mainly farmers and Serbs in the former Habsburg provinces who all supported the centralized kingdom of Serbian King Alexander. Croats overwhelmingly supported the Croatian Peasant Party, led by Stjepan Radic, a controversial and obstructionistic personality, and president of the Moscow-sponsored Peasant International. In the political life of Yugoslavia, Radic wanted Croatia to retain its identity as a "peasant republic."

To bolster Yugoslavia's external security, Alexander made efforts to ally his new nation with France, and also formed the Little Entente alliance with Czechoslovakia and Romania. Internally, the political turmoil did not subside.

Serbo-Croatian confrontations intensified, and in 1928 Stjepan Radic was seriously wounded in the Yugoslav parliament chamber by a Serb delegate from Montenegro, Punisa Racic. The crisis was at its peak. To prevent further political turmoil and to consolidate Yugoslavia internally, King Alexander dissolved the parliament and took the reigns of power into his own hands. The abolition of political parties almost destroyed the political system and the parties, particularly in Serbia. Alexander's efforts to recruit prominent Serbian and Croatian political personalities to participate in his government brought no results.

In 1934, while on an official visit to France, King Alexander was assassinated by Croatian-inspired terrorists hoping to destabilize the kingdom and accelerate the secession. The Karadjordjevic family, however, preserved power as Prince Paul Karadjordjevic, first cousin of Alexander, became regent, ruling on behalf of Alexander's son, Peter II, who was too young to assume the throne. Yugoslavia continued its tortuous existence as a new parliament struggled to find a solution to Serbo-Croatian disagreements.

Following Alexander's death, Yugoslavia remained isolated. Except for Greece, it was surrounded by countries linked with the Axis. In December 1940, Hitler issued directives for the invasion of the Soviet Union. In the meantime, he helped Mussolini conquer Greece, while Bulgaria agreed to a German military presence on its territory. Simultaneously, British troops started arriving in Greece. Hitler could not allow Britain to consolidate its military foothold in that country, but before he could take any action against Greece, he needed to clarify Yugoslavia's position. Yugoslav Prime Minister Dragisa Cvetkovic visited Hitler in mid-February 1941, at which time Hitler offered to guarantee Yugoslavia's integrity, while asserting that Germany would not ask for military cooperation. Although Prince Paul's sympathies lay on the side of Britain, he gave in to practical necessity. As war appeared more imminent in Central Europe, Prince Paul was in no position to bring attention to his country's military weakness. On March 25, 1941, Yugoslavia signed the Axis anti-Comintern Pact with Germany, Italy, and Japan, which was interpreted as surrendering to Germany. The pact contained a secret protocol saying that nothing was expected of Yugoslavia except strict neutrality -- no passage of troops, no military assistance or responsibilities. However, signing the pact triggered considerable unrest in Serbia and caused a military putsch on March 27, 1941. Prince Paul left the country as the military coup overthrew the Yugoslav government and proclaimed King Peter of age. British Prime Minister Winston Churchill welcomed the coup and declared that Yugoslavia had found its soul.

Undaunted, Hitler considered Yugoslavia an obstacle to the realization of his plans against Greece and the Soviet Union. On April 6, claiming abuse of a German minority in the Yugoslav province of Vojvodina, Hitler attacked Yugoslavia without declaring war. Belgrade was heavily bombed for three days, and the poorly equipped and unprepared Yugoslav army surrendered after only a few weeks. King Peter and the government retreated to London while the Axis powers proceeded to devour Yugoslavia.

By 1942, Germany had occupied the entire Balkan region in its push eastward into Russia. Axis forces conquered Yugoslavia, Greece, and Albania, while Romania and Bulgaria joined the Axis alignment. Yugoslavia was dissected. Germany and Italy split Slovenia, Italy seized parts of Dalmatia, Bulgaria annexed most of Macedonia, and Albania took Kosovo and Metohija on behalf of Italy. Hungary assumed a large part of northern Serbia, known today as the Province of Vojvodina, while Serbia itself was occupied by German forces and partly self-administered by a local government. Excessive punitive measures against the Serbian population (e.g. 100 Serbs were shot whenever a German soldier was killed by the resistance) were the major factor in general Milan Nedic's decision to come back from a POW camp to head the local Serbian government.

In Croatia and Bosnia-Herzegovina, Germany established a fascist "Independent State of Croatia" and set up a puppet government under Ante Pavelic, the leader of the Croatian Ustashi party. This puppet state declared war against the United States on December 8, 1941.

Subsequent harsh German occupational politics and dissatisfaction among Serbs, because of the speedy defeat, gave early rise to Serb national resistance movements. The first guerrilla movement in Europe against Nazi Germany was initiated by the followers of Yugoslav Royal Army Colonel Draza Mihailovic. Known as Chetniks, and almost exclusively composed of Serbs in Serbia, Croatia and Bosnia-Herzegovina, they fought against the Ustashi and against Tito's Communist Partisans. The Ustashi, Croat clones of the German SS, supported by Germany, Italy and Hungary, massacred hundreds of thousands of Serbs, Jews and Gypsies in the course of the war. Their intent was to eliminate the Serbian population in Croatia and Bosnia-Herzegovina. The official policy conceived by the Croat minister of Education and Culture, Milo Budak, and conducted by the Croatian government was to deport one-third of the Serbs, convert one-third to Roman Catholicism and liquidate the remaining third.

World War II in Yugoslavia was not only a struggle against the Nazis, but also a civil war between the Serbs, Croats and Bosnian Moslems. By the end of 1943, Western allies abandoned General Mihailovic and his predominantly Serbian Yugoslav Army in the Homeland and switched their support to Tito's Partisans. They were mostly Serbs, but from the areas of Yugoslavia with few if any of Mihailovic's troops, e.g., Croatia, Western Bosnia and Dalmatia.

An allied decision sealed the postwar fate of Yugoslavia. At the end of the war Tito and his Partisans gained control over Yugoslavia with Western and Soviet help and set up a comprehensive, all-pervasive Communist system.

TITO: THE FATHER OF THE SECOND YUGOSLAVIA

Napoleon said that every soldier carried a marshal's scepter in his knapsack. Josip Broz Tito, a poorly educated waiter and locksmith from Croatia, served in several armies before succeeding in becoming a Communist leader. Tito was a junior sergeant in the Austro-Hungarian army on the eastern front in World War I. He was a prisoner of war in Russia during the October Revolution in 1917. Although he never admitted it, there are indications that he was also involved in the Spanish Civil War. His rise to apotheosis began in the World War II as commander of the Partisans. During the war, he led the fight against the Germans and against the Serbian resistance, the legal successor of the annihilated Yugoslav royal army. Thanks to the allies, at the end of World War II Marshal Tito was the new Yugoslav leader and supreme commander of a Yugoslav army that was estimated to be more numerous than the British army. He ruled Yugoslavia for the next thirty-five years with an iron-hand. There was no denazification, and the war crime trials that were organized were primarily politically motivated. The "harmony" among Yugoslav nationalities was perfect. "Brotherhood and Unity" was forever, or so he hoped.

Tito was the sixth child of a large but poor peasant family in Kumrovac, some 30 miles northwest of Zagreb. Tito's birthday was celebrated in Yugoslavia on May 25 as "a day of Youth," but church books and other documents show other dates of birth. The differences were explained by the need to conspire, a practice that dominated a good portion of his life as a Communist conspirator. Many other details of his private life remained unknown even after his death. Various biographers have claimed that he was married as many as sixteen times. State records show he was married only three times.

How Tito became the main leader of the Yugoslav Communists is still a puzzle. Only after his death did some chroniclers claim that Tito gave four different accounts of the events surrounding the Stalinist-style purges within the Yugoslav Communist Party that in 1937 led to his rise to power. Throughout his reign, Tito skillfully rid himself of anybody he perceived to be a competitor. Among them were Montenegrin ideologist and Politburo member Milovan Djilas (removed in 1954), Serbian Minister of the Interior Aleksandar Rankovic (removed in 1966) and local Croatian nationalist leaders Mika Tripalo and Savka Dabcevic-Kucar (removed in 1971). Others included Macedonian leader Krste Crvenkovski, Serbian leaders Latinka Perovic and Marko Nikezic (removed in 1972), as well as others who headed the Serbian Communist Reformist movement.

Except for Djilas, all of the deposed accepted their removal in a disciplined manner, with statements of loyalty. In return, they were not persecuted or jailed, but quietly became *non-personae*. It was prohibited to write or talk about them, unless they were making public statements or involved in politics. Djilas, however, was a long-time leading dissident who refused to keep quiet. His defiance landed him in jail, where he spent a number of years.

Throughout his reign as an infallible arbiter of internal problems, Tito became much more oriented toward international politics. He gained his international standing as a result of two events. In 1948, Tito's successful resistance to Stalin's threat and intimidations gained him independence from the Soviet bloc. In 1956, joining with India's Prime Minister, Jawaharlal Nehru and Egypt's President Gamal Abdal Nasser, Tito helped found the Nonaligned Movement, a formidable group of leaders of Third-World countries. Their efforts sought to gain for their countries greater independence from the superpowers and yet retain their good will with respect to economic assistance and assurances against neocolonialism.

From the American perspective, Tito's strength was his ability to create a schism in the Communist world. The United States respected his courage in opposing the Soviets. The Soviet Union attempted on several occasions to return Yugoslavia to its orbit after their break in 1948, but Tito refused to surrender his precious independence. To him, the independence he gained from the Soviet bloc was more beneficial than any of the assets that would have come his way as a state leader under Moscow's umbrella. His regime, however, remained as oppressive as any other Communist rule, except for some privileges that Yugoslavs enjoyed, e.g., Yugoslavs could travel abroad virtually as they pleased.

The only world leader who appeared to show no respect for Tito or Yugoslavia was French President Charles De Gaulle, but his animosity was personal, not political. Draza Mihailovic, the Serbian resistance leader and rival of Tito's during World War II, was De Gaulle's classmate at the French military academy of Saint-Cyr. At the end of the war, Tito had General Mihailovic executed, and after that nothing could compel De Gaulle to meet with the man he blamed for the unjust death of a friend.

TITO'S PERSONALITY

Tito is often credited with being the only leader in Eastern Europe to bring the Communist party to power without the help of Soviet tanks and keep it in power in spite of them. Nevertheless, the fact remains that the Soviet Red Army extended crucial military assistance to Tito in 1944-45. Beginning in the late 1950s and the early 1960s, however, Yugoslavs got a glimpse of liberalizing changes. Thanks to Western aid the economy improved, and citizens were allowed to travel abroad. This created opportunities for temporary employment in the West, especially in West Germany, where rapid economic growth had caused a labor shortage.

At the onset of the World War II, Tito relied on skillful propaganda to create for himself a cult of personality. Such propaganda, which among other things later praised him for bringing a fairly good standard of living to Yugoslavia, contributed to his domestic popularity. He was a war victor, a builder of a new peaceful socialist society, and a successful strategist of the Nonaligned Movement. He received tributes from Moscow and from the West, which extended him material and political support for his independent stance -- a total of $102 billion, including $36 billion from the US alone.

Tito's personality was shrewdly combined with an inherent Balkan need to adore the chief of state. But he also took advantage of a communist system that relied heavily on the cult of personality. Only a few dissidents, like Milovan Djilas, questioned that image.

After Tito's death, as opponents began to break down the strong political barriers that existed while he ruled, legal barriers were adopted to protect his reputation and authority posthumously. Belgrade poet Gojko Djogo was jailed in 1985 for writing poems that allegedly depicted the late president as a tyrant. But with Djogo's trial came the first revelations explicitly and sensationally unveiling previously unknown sides of Tito's character. Political underlings from Tito's inner circle described his life as a feudal court where the word of the sovereign was the measure of truth and justice. These accusations differed significantly from the official hymns of praise and propaganda, but they reinforced another part of Tito's image that he had also cultivated -- that of a nouveau riche who had a weakness for luxury, bourgeois manners and a taste for trashy works of art.

Memoirs and documents found in the federal archives suggest that the people surrounding Tito were not any better. His post-war spouse, Jovanka, a Serb from Croatia and a Partisan major, had been accused of having a despotic attitude toward servants, for participating behind the scenes in political and personnel decisions and for having even more serious political ambitions during Tito's advanced age. Tito spent the last years of his life separated, but not divorced from his wife.

Some of the most serious but unsubstantiated accusations against Jovanka concerned her relationship with Ivan Krajacic-Stevo, one of the most mysterious personalities of the Yugoslav Communist movement. Krajacic, a Croatian leader, who some believed was an agent of the Comintern, was one of the very few men who could speak on an equal footing with Tito in a free and open manner. He gained Tito's trust allegedly by refusing a Comintern order to murder his boss, and instead confided in him, sparing his life.

The closeness that Krajacic enjoyed with Tito proved to be nearly untouchable when Krajacic openly told some Serbian war veterans that it was too bad that more Serbs were not killed in the concentration camp in Jasenovac during the war. Only his close relationship with the Marshal could explain his being forgiven for such a political *faux pas*. Tito also had more confidence in those Yugoslav Communists who had likewise spent time in Moscow. Only those communists who had not completed their political education in Moscow, such as Djilas and Serbian police chief Aleksandar Rankovic, among others, fell into Tito's disfavor. On the other hand, Moscow-educated politicians such as the second in command to Tito, Slovene Edvard Kardelj, and Croatian President Vladimir Bakaric spent the rest of their lives as members of his inner circle.

In an effort to win favor with the uncrowned king, each Yugoslav republic had created separate, luxurious residences and hunting grounds in the most beautiful places for use only by Tito. The largest and the best known was the archipelago Brioni, in the northern Adriatic, which was transformed into a large resort for state activities and Tito's own personal enjoyment. He readily used the isolated resort in moments of political crises. It was there that he held secret talks with the Soviet Premier Nikita Khrushchev, who briefed him and asked for his advice about the intended invasion of Hungary in 1956. Ten years later, a meeting was held there that resulted in the ousting of police chief Rankovic, who was accused of excessive use of his interior police power. Tito's security was maintained by the army, not the police units, and Rankovic was accused of installing listening devices in Tito's office and bedroom. The affair was investigated by a special group loyal to Tito zealot Ivan Krajacic, who ultimately removed Rankovic.

Another favorite resort of Tito's was Brdo kod Kranja, a mountainous Slovenian resort of Austrian nobility, whose last owner was Serbian Prince Paul Karadjordjevic. Still another favorite was "Karadjordjevo," a hunting ground in the Vojvodina plains near Belgrade, which was frequently used for political meetings and for the hunting parties of foreign dignitaries and diplomats.

Since Tito's death, not much has been done with the state property that he used as his own. Unsuccessful attempts have been made to sell some of his belongings, including his famous Blue Train, composed of two locomotives and twenty cars, with an estimated value of forty million dollars. The Yugoslav government has also been unable to find much of the art collection, including works by Rembrandt, that Tito pilfered from original owners. Some of Tito's properties that have been sold or allocated to republics are being used as hotels or resorts. In addition to the government's interest in Tito's estate, his wife Jovanka and his sons Zarko and Aleksandar initiated a lawsuit against the state, demanding a larger share of Tito's assets. That lawsuit is still pending but the outcome of it is uncertain due to the ongoing civil war.

Official propaganda "classified" Tito's character traits so that everyone was able to identify with him in some way. He was depicted as a hunter, fisherman, beekeeper, pianist, chess player, fruit grower and lover of animals. Beyond that, he was an admirer of motion pictures (especially Western movies) and a friend of famous personalities in the art world. By deeds and association, Tito was made out to be a universally superhuman being, an image that he seemed to enjoy. In addition to the glitter that surrounded him at home, he traveled extensively. He enjoyed sailing his yacht all around the world, accompanied by three naval destroyers.

While he was alive, volumes of apologetic books were written about him, but since his death, many books and critiques have offered previously untold and unflattering apocryphal tales. Several best sellers in Yugoslavia brought out the "dirty laundry" and sensational details of Tito's inclination toward luxuries and privileges.

TITOISM

"Titoism" was the label coined to describe Yugoslavia's distinct path to socialism. Domestically, at the beginning it was marked by the Soviet-style collectivization that turned confiscated individual farms into huge state enterprises. Yugoslav socialism was an "experimental laboratory" that introduced workers self-management. Highly publicized and often praised by Yugoslavs as well as the West as an original concept, it brought into managerial positions workers who often collided on management decisions, causing conflicts and a poor decision-making process. Without real owners and responsible management, those enterprises were unproductive and gradually terminated. This type of socialism did allow for small-scale private property with ultimate control still in the hands of the party, which was always ready to intervene to prevent individuals from acquiring wealth and inordinate power that would threaten the ruling structure.

After breaking with Moscow in 1948, Tito succeeded in maintaining an open relationship with both the East and the West. He believed that "nonalignment" was the 20th-century answer to old fashioned neutrality, and thus helped to establish the Nonaligned Movement, which brought him publicity and prestige on the world stage, but ultimately only insignificant economic and practical gains. Tito perceived nonalignment as being less isolationist and more active, especially in reconciling the differences between West and East. The first conference of nonaligned countries, in Belgrade in 1961, adopted policies that had certain influence in world politics in the 1960s and 1970s.

TITO'S ROLE IN INTER-ETHNIC RELATIONS

During World War II, the Croatian Ustashi forces, like Nazi Germany, found themselves fighting against, and ultimately losing to, a Communist movement that advocated a heterogeneous Yugoslavia. Serbian patriots fighting against the Communists also tried unsuccessfully to institute their own government. After the war, the Communists carried out a policy of artificial equality among Yugoslav nationalities. Unlike Russians in the Soviet Union, Serbs did not enjoy any extra power or political privileges as a result of their being the largest ethnic group in a new Communist, multinational state. In fact, many Serbs still feel a sense of oppression, brought on by Tito -- a Croat -- and his anti-Serbian policies.

The Yugoslav Communist Party, with many Serbian members, had been active as early as 1919, but before World War II, Serbs did not have their own national Communist organization, while the Croats and Slovenes did. Some experts claim that Moscow's mistrust of Serbs could be explained at the time by an apparent anti-Communist orientation among the Serbs.

The determination of internal borders following World War II also showed signs of discrimination against Serbs. They did not resemble previous ethnic or historic considerations, and were ultimately decided only on Tito's final authority. Jovan Veselinov, the long-time Communist leader in the Serbian province of Vojvodina, admitted to Serbian acquiescence to the new administrative lines, which he said were established to unite more than separate, because Serbs wanted to keep peace in what they figured to be a united state. The redrawn borders were a particular point of contention when Croatia, Slovenia and Bosnia-Herzegovina moved to establish their own republics, at the expense of what Serbia saw as its original borders when it entered the union in 1918.

Serbia was also the only republic during the Communist reorganization of the post-war state to be partitioned into autonomous provinces. Protecting ethnic-minority rights, the logic used to establish the autonomous provinces of Vojvodina and Kosovo for ethnic-Hungarians and ethnic-Albanians, respectively, could also have been justified for ethnic-Serbs in the Croatian region of Slavonija and Krajina. The same "Vojvodina" logic could have been applied to the Croatian region of Dalmatia as well, which historically had autonomous status and included ethnic-Italians and ethnic-Serbs living among the Croats. Likewise, Bosnia-Herzegovina, with its mixed population of Serbs, Croats and Moslems, could also have been divided into autonomous provinces, well before the republic was torn apart by war.

After World War II, ethnic-Germans who fought for and collaborated with the Nazis were not forcibly moved out of Vojvodina, while Tito encouraged the emigration of the Italians in Istria and Dalmatia. Hungarians and Albanians, however, a majority of whom also collaborated with Germany, were encouraged to stay in Vojvodina and Kosovo. This was Tito's way of keeping the Serbian lands ethnically diluted.

In another ambiguous demographic move, this one possibly aimed at Serbian industry, in 1948 Tito ordered the transfer of numerous Serbian factories to Slovenia. The move was explained by the vulnerability of Serbia to Soviet troops if Stalin decided to attack Yugoslavia. The strategy, it was argued, was to concentrate industry in the western portions of the country.

Tito's impartiality was also called into question by his choice of authors of Yugoslavia's several post-war constitutions. At least two of those constitutions, heavily favoring confederation over federation, were penned by Tito collaborators Edvard Kardelj, a

Slovenian primary school teacher and failed journalist and Vladimir Bakaric, a fellow Croat.

However, to emphasize his genuine belief in federalism, regardless of ethnicity, Tito forcibly intimidated Slovenian and Croatian nationalist movements at the end of the 1960s and the beginning of the 1970s. A few years later, seemingly only to further his appearance of even-handedness, he also removed the entire Communist leadership of the Serbian republic.

Upon his death, Tito was praised as the father of the Yugoslav wonder, but as early as the mid 1970s, Serbian intellectuals began openly criticizing Tito's policies. This later became more open through a highly critical Slovenian press and other media outlets. Other republics, however, remained quiet or, as in the case of Bosnia-Herzegovina, insisted on carrying out Titoism. His photographs decorated offices all across Yugoslavia throughout the 1980s. Not until the fall of 1991 did Serbian school officials remove Tito's picture from the cover of school textbooks, replacing it with a portrait of Vuk Karadzic, the nineteenth-century father of the modern Serbian alphabet and phonetic Cyrillic writing style.

In the exclusive Belgrade neighborhood of Dedinje, behind the high walls of the fashionable Uzicka Street, lies the tomb of Marshal Josip Broz Tito. The founder of the second Yugoslavia is buried in the yard of his villa, in what was once a green house. It is an ideal setting for contemplation, a majestic surrounding of greenery that shows no sign of the destroyed state that followed in the wake of Tito's death. For years after his death, long lines of visitors and tourists waited, either out of respect or curiosity, to see the final resting place of the leader who created the special brand of communism that kept the unlikely state together for over three and a half decades. On his grave there is neither a cross nor a Communist five-pointed star. Some speculate that the lack of markings gives credence to the belief that Tito was actually a Mason, the only group in Yugoslavia buried without any symbols other than a name. Other Serbian opposition parties want the tomb moved to Croatia, arguing that Tito's discrimination against Serbs makes him unworthy of a final resting place in the Serbian capital. It is not a coincidence that Serbs today are some of the most open and outspoken critics of Tito.

AFTER TITO: BURGEONING ECONOMIC AND POLITICAL CRISES

In 1982, only two years after Tito's death, a world debt crisis erupted, showing, much to the surprise of Yugoslavs, that Yugoslavia was one of the most indebted countries in the world. People did not understand how the country could be so poor. It was a country with a high standard of living, one that enabled them to enjoy the 1970s by shopping in Italy, vacationing in Greece and the French Riviera, and skiing in Austria and Switzerland. What was not obvious to the average citizen, however, was that there were few reasons to be proud of the effectiveness of their country's economy or organization. The unusually high standard of living for a Communist country was not due to an effective socialist self-managing system, but rather inexpensive Western credits granted to federal authorities, republics, even individual firms. And such poor records were kept that it was not even known who owed how much of the debt, or to whom. Following the prosperity of the 1970s, there was a rude awakening. All that remained for Yugoslavia after Tito was a bill for the unpaid foreign credits that created the illusion of prosperity and social tranquillity.

Following Tito's death, the country's leadership was not able to hold the country together. Economic problems started influencing the already-sensitive ethnic relations. The leadership's answer, however, was more of the same. It was unable or unwilling, to design anything new, something to move away from the framework that it inherited.

The first violence after Tito's death occurred in 1981 in the troubled province of Kosovo. Ethnic Albanians demanded a separate republic, even though the 1974 federal constitution granted them far reaching autonomy, essentially the same autonomy as the republics. The leadership of Kosovo had almost unlimited power inside Kosovo as well as proportional influence in the Yugoslav federation, with two representatives in the federal presidency, where most major issues were decided by consensus. The Serbian fear behind formal autonomy for Kosovo was that it was a prelude to secession and eventually unification with Albania.

Demonstrations in Kosovo were crushed by a still-effective and disciplined Communist party in the region that was not afraid to use force. Predictions of further unrest and even more unsettling times, however, were safe and accurate. An incompetent Yugoslav and Serbian leadership attempted to simply sweep the trouble under the rug. Without much protest, the Albanian leadership in Kosovo was able to continue the repression of Serbian and Montenegrin ethnic minorities, including destruction of property and other violence committed, encouraged, or covered up by ethnic-Albanians, their politicians and groups of corrupt Serbs working for them. Their cause was aided by a generally ineffective and paralyzed legal system.

THE YUGOSLAV FEDERAL GOVERNMENT

During his reign, Tito and his closest associates were untouchable arbiters. The foremost of these associates was the Slovene and long-time second in command, Edvard Kardelj. His other favorites rotated their positions. According to the 1974 Constitution, which Tito promulgated, the collective presidency held formal power only as long as Tito was alive and gave full independence to the Yugoslav republics, encouraging separatist tendencies and the eventual collapse of Yugoslavia. The functioning of the collective presidency afterwards also proved inept because of a one-year time limit on power, and because of the inexperience or unwillingness of some of the unknown politicians sent by the republics to govern at the highest levels. Such was the case in 1989 when the Slovenian representative,

Janez Drnovsek, became head of the presidency, despite his dissatisfaction with the federation.

While Drnovsek at least had the support of his republic, political clashes in Bosnia-Herzegovina brought to the federal presidency a Serb, Bogic Bogicevic, who did not even have grassroots support from the Bosnian Serbs, much less the other nationalities in the republic. Other republics sent similarly weak political personalities, which only indicated that the center of power remained in the republics, and that the federal presidency was supposed to serve only as a forum for political conflicts among the republics. In the international political arena, foreign dignitaries had trouble remembering the name of the chief of the Yugoslav state as the position rotated annually. This also precluded long-lasting or close relationships on the international scene.

Infighting among the members of the Federal Executive Council reached its most dramatic levels under Prime Minister Ante Markovic, who came to power in January 1989 following the resignation of the government of Branko Mikulic. Markovic was faced with an economic crisis and difficulties in implementing a uniform program for the entire country. From the very beginning, however, Markovic was able to get international support for developing a reform plan that was considered one of the most progressive in Eastern Europe at the time. Already having what was seen as the most market-oriented economy in Eastern Europe, under Markovic Yugoslavia was able to get new aid packages from the World Bank and the International Monetary Fund.

With the help of the two international financial institutions, along with the European Community and Washington, Ante Markovic succeeded in starting the wheels of the Yugoslav economic machine and stopping a galloping inflation that had reached a yearly rate of 2000 percent. The heavy price that reform entailed, however, only further deteriorated an already fragile federal government. Serbia objected to the anti-Serbian tendencies of the federal government, while Slovenia and Croatia hampered most federal efforts by maintaining only minimal rules that applied to the entire country.

Markovic, a Croat, had been hailed as a political and economic reformer, even though he assumed the premiership without being elected. As a long-time Communist technocrat, Markovic worked his way up through the party's leadership, only to disavow Yugoslavia's need for the Communist party at the 14th Party Congress in late 1990, after his government fell. His efforts to reform a federal government that was dissolving underneath him, as the individual republics withdrew their support, alienated him from republican leaders across the spectrum. His policies even seemed to temporarily unite irreconcilable opponents Slobodan Milosevic and Franjo Tudjman in an unsuccessful effort to oust him.

With leaders who were simply representatives of their respective republican governments, individual interests clashed head on in March 1991, when Serbia and Montenegro, with the help of the army, tried unsuccessfully to impose martial law. It appears their intention was to disarm separatist-minded military units forming in Slovenia and Croatia, which the other republics perceived as a military coup. However, the military units were indeed created with the intent to secede and, if necessary, engage in war.

Markovic's government was the last one formed during one-party Communist rule. Despite his economic reforms, which brought the country's inflation under control, his political reforms proved to be his downfall, as his fledgling Reformist Party could not stand up to the Communists in multi-party elections. The Reformists had moderate electoral success only in Macedonia and Montenegro, and failed in every other republic. National and local passions outweighed any support for the government's reform program. Despite strong outside support for the reforms of the federal government, actions to incapacitate the system prevailed.

First Slovenia and Croatia withdrew their recognition of the central government's authority, and later Serbia joined them, believing that it too was at times handicapped by federal decisions. Republican leaders found confrontation with the federal government to be a source of support for them at home, and it gave them a scapegoat for the regional economic problems pressing their populations. The separatist-minded republics sent a message that by seceding from Yugoslavia all problems would be solved. The government's late attempt to form its own political party, after the elections in Slovenia and Croatia, met with little success. Nobody seemed interested in having a government form a political party, instead of the other way around. Markovic's Reformists were also not ready to represent local interests, the support of which was mandatory for success.

THE YUGOSLAV PEOPLE'S ARMY

The Yugoslav People's Army was created from Communist guerrilla units, known as Partisans who fought the Nazis during World War II. At the same time, the Partisans also fought against the Serbian anti-fascist Chetnik forces in Yugoslavia's civil war. Winston Churchill convinced the allies that Tito's Partisans were fighting more efficiently than the Chetniks, and therefore should be sent aid. When asked if he thought that aid to the Partisans would result in the Communists coming to power, Churchill cynically replied that he did not intend to live in Yugoslavia.

With a strength of over 700,000 troops during the immediate post-war period, all the ranks of the army from the officers on down were systematically indoctrinated with Communist theory and subjected to Communist practices by Tito. These military practices lasted the entire time the Communists were in power, but for the most part the army was relegated to the formal protection of the regime, and did not have a significant influence on the country's politics.

Buoyed with the confidence of being a winning army at the end of World War II, the Yugoslav army undertook what it considered to be its three main tasks: first, the defense of the country regardless of the enemy; second, a cultivation of the absolute and unconditional obedience and loyalty to Tito; and third, the maintenance of a balance between all Yugoslav peoples and ethnic groups in the army and the rest of the country. Most likely because of a strong military tradition in Serbia, and the numerical advantage of Serbs in the Yugoslav population, they made up the bulk of the army's officer corps. Despite persistent efforts to recruit other nationalities into its ranks, by offering relatively high salaries and modest but not extravagant benefits, the army always had what it considered a shortage of mixed nationalities. However, senior officers were chosen not only for their national background, but also because of their faithfulness to communism and Yugoslavism.

Some 80 percent of the Yugoslav army's arms were produced in the country. Aircraft were mostly purchased from the Soviet Union, while most of the electronics were imported from the United States. The Yugoslav military-industrial complex produced a considerable number of arms on foreign consignment, some of which were exported to Arab and African countries. Others were even sold to American armed forces stationed in Europe. Yugoslav-built, Soviet-licensed M-84 tanks also made up part of the allied armament in the Persian Gulf War.

Despite being one of the best trained armed forces in Eastern Europe, the Yugoslav army never considered the possibility of needing to take action against its own people, independent of foreign intervention. Separatist tendencies were analyzed within the military doctrine only in the context of an attack by an external enemy. During longtime Communist rule, in a country that offered a relatively comfortable standard of living and did not allow any opposition, internal political dissension that could lead to war was simply not thought possible. This opinion was furthered by the government's constant encouragement and celebration of unity between the army and the country's various ethnic groups. But, as Yugoslavia started disintegrating and Slovenia and Croatia created their own national armies, Serbia, however reluctantly, took the path of using the Serbian army for the defense of its national interests.

YUGOSLAVIA: THE WILD CARD OF INTERNATIONAL POLITICS

THE POST-WAR RELATIONSHIP WITH MOSCOW

Relations between the Soviet Union and Yugoslavia were at their apex right after World War II. Yugoslavia's Communists saw in Moscow an example that they thought should be followed. Close economic and political cooperation, along with obsequious affection toward Stalin by the Yugoslav leadership, lasted until 1948. Tito began to realize that Stalin would not tolerate the creation of a second cult of personality within his sphere of influence, and the secretary-general of the Yugoslav Communist Party presumed his removal was forthcoming. But Tito was able to use his relatively strong military as insurance against anything that threatened his hold on power. In this effort, he was also backed by an indirect connection to NATO through a tripartite defense treaty with Greece and Turkey, and a strong enough economy to endure his break in 1948 from Moscow and the rest of Eastern Europe.

Severing relations with the Communist bloc, however, did not induce Tito and his inner circle of leaders to steer away from a Communist system within Yugoslavia. Confiscation and nationalization of private property and businesses before the split with Stalin was continued in the early 1950s, even though it was having a negative effect on Yugoslavia's economy. During the war, industry had been almost destroyed, but many peasants still were able to farm successfully. Federal authorities, however, used the Soviet model of "Kolhozes" as a basis for forcibly expropriating agricultural land and products. This centralized agricultural policy took all momentum away from the prosperous farming sector and led to a progressively stagnant output, so that it was eventually discontinued.

At the same time, to show its distance and to protect itself from Stalin's regime, Tito's government jailed Yugoslavia's most prominent supporters of the Soviet Union. Those considered the worst offenders -- numbering in the thousands of mostly Serbs and Montenegrins -- were sent to a forced labor camp on the Adriatic island of Goli Otok. The physical and psychological conditions of Goli Otok rivaled Stalin's gulags and provided a horrific backdrop for all sorts of writings once Tito died.

The death of Stalin in 1953, did not completely mend Yugoslav-Soviet relations, but tension was reduced, particularly after First Secretary Nikita Khrushchev visited Belgrade in 1955. Tito and Khrushchev signed the Belgrade declaration, which recognized the sovereignty and equality of both states. Khrushchev admitted that Stalin had unjustly condemned Tito, and a year later Tito visited Moscow. But relations between the two countries remained reserved, as Yugoslavs continued to question Moscow's stated intentions regarding Yugoslav-Soviet relations. Belgrade found what it thought to be evidence for its reservations when Soviet tanks rolled into Budapest in 1956 to violently crush Hungary's anti-Communist revolt.

At its Seventh Party Congress in 1958, the Yugoslav leadership adopted a definitively different brand of communism. Relatively decentralized power was instituted, and the Communist party assumed a less exposed role within the state. Following the Congress, certain forms of strictly controlled democracy were introduced, and agricultural activity was increasingly liberalized. However, many prohibitions remained in place, such as bans on political opposition and a free press, but Yugoslavia was nonetheless moving in its own direction.

The direction in which Tito was headed was cooperation with the newly independent developing countries. The tripartite cooperation among Tito, Egyptian President Gemal Abdel Nasser and Indian Premier Jawaharlal Nehru served as the embryo of what would become known as the Nonaligned Movement, which advocated an approach to international relations independent of both superpowers. But as the outlook of member countries ranged from pro-Western to Soviet-client status, usually depending on who was providing them aid, the Nonaligned Movement met every three years, mostly to take firm stances only on issues such as anticolonialism, which would not jeopardize the material interests of their dependent economies.

A relatively tolerant relationship between Yugoslavia and the Soviet Union lasted until 1968, when Soviet forces once again intervened in Central Europe, this time in Czechoslovakia. Yugoslavs showed a great affinity toward the regime of Aleksander Dubcek, which put them at odds with Soviet leader Leonid Brezhnev. After the invasion of Czechoslovakia, Brezhnev formulated a theory of "limited sovereignty," which meant that Soviet troops could intervene in other socialist countries if they determined that Communist rule or Soviet interests were endangered.

Yugoslavia considered Brezhnev's theory a direct threat to its sovereignty. The Soviet invasion of Czechoslovakia triggered a limited mobilization in Yugoslavia, which showed how unprepared the Yugoslav army actually was to withstand a possible attack. This realization led to the incorporation of Yugoslavia's existing regular army with official guerrilla units and units of civil defense in order to shore up its defense against any possible foreign intervention. The strength of these combined federal forces grew over the years, but as the core of the federation began to splinter, so too did various guerrilla units, which later developed into paramilitary units within individual republics.

As a leader of the Nonaligned Movement, Yugoslavia was even more concerned by Moscow's invasion of one of the movement's members, Afghanistan. In practical terms, Belgrade considered the 1979 invasion one of the strongest threats to the independence of the Third World movement, and in ideological terms it was seen as yet another demonstration of Brezhnev's theory of limited sovereignty, which Yugoslavia also opposed.

Independent of the artificial affection Yugoslavia's Communists demonstrated toward Stalin immediately following World War II, and the increased economic cooperation between the two countries in the late 1970s, no Soviet leader really appealed to Yugoslavs until Mikhail Gorbachev aroused their interest when he came to power in 1985. During his visit to Belgrade, in 1989, Gorbachev took advantage of the occasion to praise the Yugoslav Communist experiment and to vow that Moscow would not attempt to interfere with the internal affairs of other socialist states.

Gorbachev's assertion that the Soviet Union would not intervene in the affairs of other countries, which later proved to be the death knell for so many Communist governments in the region, mitigated any complimentary or obligatory references he made at the time to the benefits of the Yugoslav brand of communism when compared to the other states of the Soviet system.

AMERICAN POLICY TOWARD YUGOSLAVIA

With the exception of the brief transitional period immediately following the end of World War II, when all political powers were sorting out their political objectives, the United States took a favorable approach to Tito's Communist regime. The United States saw an independent and strong Yugoslavia as not only a suitable buffer state against the more totalitarian regimes to the east, but Tito was also seen as an example that could be flaunted in front of the Soviet empire as a viable alternative to Stalinism. Any potential schisms within the international Communist system could then be exacerbated by the United States with continued support for Yugoslav positions.

Tito, however, was well aware of his value in the balance of power and depending on his needs was adept at playing his hand in favor of Washington or Moscow, often at the expense of damaging U.S.-Yugoslav relations. Paradoxically, during and after Tito's reign, as increasing democracy, free elections and greater freedom of the press evolved in Yugoslavia, the list of American objections to Yugoslav human rights violations grew longer than ever. The evolving supposition was that U.S. support for democracy in Yugoslavia was far more theoretical than practical. Despite a facade of democratic reform, Tito's real ideological strength expressed itself in his stewardship of the Nonaligned Movement, which former Secretary of State John Foster Dulles once called amoral.

Just as apparent policy contradictions by Tito worked to confound successive U.S. administrations, recent diplomatic efforts on the part of Congress and the Reagan and Bush administrations left political leaders in Belgrade equally confused. Yugoslav politicians, particularly Serbians, could not reconcile the two foremost elements of the U.S. policy toward Yugoslavia -- namely, the initial support for a united Yugoslav state and the request for further protection against human rights abuses in Kosovo. To Belgrade, any type of Western support for the ethnic Albanians in Kosovo was nothing more than support for the Albanian separatist movement. Regardless of whether or not the United States saw its interests as compatible, in the minds of Serbians the ultimate aim was a more independent Kosovo. This led to certain anti-American sentiment, which the Communists manipulated with great effectiveness, further entrenching them and further polarizing the other republics' views of the Belgrade government. Serbia's Communists hoped to be able to continue their practice of appeasing the United States by democratizing their own political system and liberalizing their economy, which had already begun adopting market reforms at the expense of human rights. But by the late

1980s, political leaders in Croatia and Slovenia had heard enough U.S. calls for a freer Kosovo to start demanding more political and social freedoms of their own.

As Congress sought to push the problems in Kosovo to the forefront of its human rights agenda in the late 1980s, lobbyists on all sides of the issue intensified their own efforts to gain support for their respective governments in Yugoslavia. The lobbying effort reached an unprecedented level with the confirmation hearings of former ambassador to Yugoslavia Lawrence Eagleburger as deputy secretary of state in March, 1989. Eagleburger, very popular while in Belgrade from 1977 to 1981, had stayed involved with U.S.-Yugoslav affairs as a member of the boards of directors of a Slovenian bank and the American branch of the Yugo car company. He was seen by the Albanian and Croatian lobbies as a barrier to their interests.

But in the hearings that led to his confirmation, Eagleburger surprised his opponents and supporters alike by advocating for the first time what would become albeit gradually the Bush administration's opinion of Yugoslavia -- that Serbian nationalism was the main source of the country's political problems. Eagleburger blamed Serbian nationalism for the treatment of ethnic-Albanians in Kosovo and pointed to the Serbian attitude as a source of fear among Slovenes and Croats, never mentioning the Croatian separatist movement of the '70s, known as Maspok, and Kardelj's continuous encouragement of separatism. When the civil war broke out, the Serbs were accused of initiating the conflict and labeled as aggressors, and never seen as a people who fought for independence and self-determination.

President Bush, however, continued to show support for the federal government of Prime Minister Ante Markovic until it fell in 1990. As Markovic's Reformist Party suffered successive defeats in multi-party elections from republic to republic, the Bush administration used that downfall as a smooth segue for a change in policy and an opportunity to more firmly embrace an anti-Milosevic stand.

Despite widespread expectations that the administration of President Clinton would adopt a more active stance than his predecessors in the conflict in Bosnia-Herzegovina, Clinton considered the Vance-Owen peace plan unjust toward Bosnian Moslems, and eventually sided openly with the Moslem cause, but avoided deeper political or military entanglement.

On February 19, 1994, President Clinton broadcast an address to the American people defining American policy in Bosnia-Herzegovina. He said that the United States has an interest in helping to prevent the Bosnian war from becoming a broader European conflict, especially one that could threaten NATO allies or undermine the transition of former Communist states to peaceful democracies. Clinton also said: "We have an interest in showing that NATO -- the world's largest military alliance -- remains a credible force in the post-cold-war era. We have an interest in helping to stem the destabilizing flows of refugees this struggle is generating throughout all of Europe. And we clearly have a humanitarian interest in helping to stop the strangulation of Sarajevo and the continuing slaughter of innocents in Bosnia. I want to be clear: Europe must bear most of the responsibility for solving this problem."

THE EUROPEAN RESPONSE TO YUGOSLAVIA

Yugoslavia proved to be the first major opportunity in the post-Communist era for the European Community and Europe's other international organizations to demonstrate how well they could handle political and military turmoil in their own territory. Europe's inconclusive response to the original political unraveling of Yugoslavia only helped to exacerbate many of the other social problems the EC found standing in the way of its building a more cohesive structure. But the pressure the Western European powers faced was not entirely self-imposed.

With each new burgeoning country throughout Europe, including all four newly independent states of the former Yugoslavia, came requests for closer ties to European political and economic organizations.

Originally, the European Community, like the United States, sought to keep Yugoslavia united, and made it clear it was only interested in offering membership to the whole country when the time came. For the EC, there were very immediate and visible reasons for wanting to prevent Yugoslavia from splitting apart. Even though secessionist movements were proliferating throughout Eastern Europe, the importance of Yugoslavia as a buffer between East and West once again came into play. Refugees looking for a haven first from economic hardship, and later war, aimed for Western Europe as the most advantageous place to take shelter. Leaders of EC countries were afraid the disintegration of Yugoslavia would not only hinder the process of unification, but would also be a harbinger of other ethnic struggles that could move Europe in the opposite direction. In addition to the push for self-determination in Eastern Europe and the former Soviet Union, there had also been independence-minded ethnic and religious movements in Spain, Belgium and northern Ireland that the European Community sought to keep in check as it continued its unification process.

Although Europe was initially for the continued existence of Yugoslavia, that attitude changed in 1991 when Germany and Austria pushed for independence and recognition of Slovenia and Croatia. In spite of the Serbo-Croat conflict that this move caused, Germany in December 1991, declared that Bonn was determined to soon recognize Bosnia-Herzegovina, an action viewed unfavorably by the Serbs, who advocated a united Yugoslavia and felt that Serbia had to protect Serbs outside its borders.

In an attempt to find a peaceful solution to the conflict in Bosnia-Herzegovina, the European Community at a meeting in Lisbon in February 1992, offered to divide the former Yugoslav republic along ethnic lines into Serbian, Croatian and Moslem regions, which was in principle accepted by all the parties. However, upon the advice of Washington, Alija Izetbegovic, the leader of Bosnian Moslems turned down this proposal.

In August 1992, at British initiative, a conference was held in London, attended by various Yugoslav parties. All of them agreed that the civil war had to be stopped, and most of the participants blamed Serbia for starting the war and being the aggressor. The London document, known as the Vance-Owen plan, made Bosnian Serbs unhappy mainly because of the following reasons: it gave only 43% of the land to them, instead of the 65% the Serbs had possessed before the civil war. In addition, Serbian land in Bosnia-Herzegovina had no continuity (connection with Krajina or Serbia proper) and the question of Bosnian Serb self-determination remained unresolved.

In July 1993, Serbs, Croats and Moslems agreed to a three-way division which Moslems rejected, after the US military threat. Subsequent US and NATO threats against Serbs encouraged Moslems to prolong the military conflict, stifling the peace process.

SERBS AND CROATS: THE KEY PLAYERS

For several years in the late 1980s and early 1990s, a very popular play titled "Chauvinist Farce" played in Belgrade with great success. It dealt with highly inflated prejudices and myths of two of the largest Yugoslav nations -- Serbs and Croats. "About two million years ago, we Serbs came from space, and then you Croats came from Iran, then came amoebas, and then other living beings," says a Serbian professor of history to his Croatian colleague in one of the play's scenes.

The line is characteristic of the Balkan mentality of measuring values and rights of a nation by the depth of the roots of its history and tradition and not by its realistic achievements, contemporary values and possible contribution of that nation to wider international communities. It is an age old argument among South Slavic nations over who came first to the Balkans and whose tribes took what regions. The quarrel is the basis upon which nations now make claims to some territories, whose ethnic composition did not altogether survive the migrations, forced and otherwise, of the past several decades.

Historic evidence to support claims for the Balkan mosaic, with the exception of the Greeks who still inhabit their ancient lands, is hard to find. Albanians claim their origin from the Illyrians, dating back to Roman times. In the 19th century, it was believed that even Slavs came from the Illyrians, a conviction so strong that the movement for the unification of South Slavs, which resulted in the creation of Yugoslavia, was termed the "Illyrian Movement."

The fictitious Serbian professor's remark about Croats' coming from Iran is not only an exaggeration and ridicule of myths, but a stab at Croatian historians who have claimed non-Slavic, "Aryan" origins for Croats. Such a notion can be traced to efforts by some Croats to push themselves farther from other Slavic peoples in the Balkans and closer to the Germans.

For centuries, cooperation and antagonism between Serbs and Croats, evidenced by a common language and culture, demonstrated the strength of their common racial roots, while confrontation existed mainly along religious lines and from the fact that they had always, until 1918, lived in different states.

Serbs and Croats are both believed to have come from the region between the river Odra in the west and the river Volga in the east, settling in the Balkans in the sixth and seventh centuries. Croats settled in the western and northern area of the peninsula. Serbs concentrated in the middle and the south of the Balkans, waging wars against Byzantium. Both groups accepted Christianity in the 9th century, but a schism within Christianity and its division into the Western Roman-Catholic Church and the Eastern Greek-Orthodox Church in the 11th century distanced Serbs from Croats.

Throughout the Middle Ages, Serbs had several separate states or one common, strong state until their defeat in the battle of Kosovo in 1389. Even after the defeat at Kosovo, Serbian rulers, as Turkish vassals, retained autonomy and statehood. Croats, however, have had a significantly shorter state history, with their only independent state being in the 10th and 11th centuries, when they merged with Hungary. Serbs and Croats fought together against the Turks, and the struggle between Christianity and Islam caused migration during which a large number of Serbs settled in the Krajina region, in the southern

35

part of the Austrian Empire. They were most often Serbs who fled Kosovo or came from other southern parts of Serbia in the 16th and 17th centuries, under Turkish pressure. They arrived as mercenaries to protect Christian Western Europe from Islamic penetration. Austria enabled them to settle in areas where Croats also settled, and they have been there ever since.

Aside from some earlier, less important conflicts, the first full-scale conflict between Croats and Serbs took place during World War I, when Croats fought as part of the Austro-Hungary Army against Serb forces. There were a few Croatian volunteers, however, who fought in the Serbian Royal Army during the war. The group of volunteers included the future Cardinal Alojzije Stepinac, who after the war become an instigator of national intolerance. He was later responsible for the forcible conversion of Serbs from the Orthodox to Catholic faith. Ivan Mestrovic, a Croat who gained fame after the war as a renowned sculptor, also fought in the Serbian army.

Although antagonism between Serbs and Croats is believed to stem from religious differences, the theoretical basis for intolerance was formed by a well known Croatian writer and 19th century politician, Ante Starcevic.

20TH CENTURY ANTAGONISM BETWEEN CROATS AND SERBS

Croats were upset with what they perceived as Serbian hegemony within the new Yugoslavia after World War I. In the years leading up to World War II, Croatian discontent was utilized by the Ustashi as justification for acts such as the assassination of King Alexander in Marseilles in 1934. When Germany, Italy, Hungary and Bulgaria occupied Yugoslavia during the World War II, the Nazis installed the Ustashi to run a puppet state. The Ustashi responded with a campaign of genocide against Serbs, Jews and Gypsies.

Croatian and Serbian estimates range from about 250,000 to 700,000 victims, respectively, at the hands of the Ustashi, and they include some of the worst atrocities committed during the war. Among a number of concentration camps, which Ustashi established, the camp at Jasenovac was especially notorious as a home for brutal torture, ruthless killing, and even the burying of healthy or wounded victims.

Communist authorities never allowed post-war investigations at Jasenovac to be completed, mass graves uncovered, or all documents to be made available. Serbs also blame Communists for not allowing their otherwise very successful guerrilla units to attempt to liberate Jasenovac. According to survivors, acts of genocide continued at Jasenovac practically until the last days of the war.

After the war, a monument, a museum and finally an Orthodox church were built at Jasenovac, but everything else that was Serbian was torn down. The Communist regime decided that destruction would be the best way to forget, or at least limit, memories of the fratricidal war in Yugoslavia, and went only as far as making general assessments. They carefully and evenly distributed guilt for the crimes committed by the Ustashi and those committed by the Serbian nationalist Chetniks. But the Communists did not reveal their own crimes, which included executions of thousands of mobilized Chetniks in Serbia and Montenegro.

Although he often traveled throughout Yugoslavia to visit historic sites, Tito never visited Jasenovac, which the Serbs considered as one of his many anti-Serbian gestures. The Communists' obfuscation of Croatian war crimes kept Croatian political leaders, even 50 years later, from acknowledging them. The first post-war, partly democratically elected government in Croatia did nothing to quiet Serbian fears, but, in fact, enhanced them.

CROATIAN NATIONALISM

While the tide of Serbian nationalism was rising in the late 1980s, in Croatia relatively fresh memories funneled its reemergence into more muted forms. In 1971, Croats were dismayed. by Tito's brutal suppression of the nationalistic movement known as Maspok. The movement was led by relatively young, prospective Communists such as Mrs. Savka Dabcevic-Kucar and Mika Tripalo, considered to be Tito's heir apparent. However, the Yugoslav constitution of 1974, granted Croatia more than it asked for during Maspok. Serbs regarded it as a renewal of the fascist Ustashi movement, while Croats saw it as a popular movement. Tito himself hesitated to undertake any action for as long as possible. He finally reacted with repressive measures by removing Dabcevic-Kucar and Tripalo, and a large number of their supporters, in order to decisively ward off any competition for power.

The Croatian leadership of the 1980s, was the same leadership Tito brought to power in the 1970s, to settle accounts with the Maspok, which probably explains why Zagreb reacted with disapproval to the developments in Serbia. Croats never perceived Slovenes as serious competition, and Slovenian nationalism enjoyed a certain sympathy in Croatia because at the time it was aimed at Serbs and the Yugoslav federation. The Croatian leadership also hesitated to take a premature position on the developments in Serbia, even though they disapproved, because Croatia had a relatively strong Serbian political movement. Prior to 1989, Croatia restrained itself from an open political war against Serbia, limiting itself to mass-media attacks.

One weapon Croatian and Slovenian companies used against Serbia was to hire Serbian politicians who had fallen from power. A defeated Serbian official who did not receive a lucrative enough offer from any of his fellow nationals, or who did not have enough capital to start his own business, knew he could count on support from the rebellious republics. The same held true for defeated Albanian politicians from Kosovo, but such "asylum" was not limited only to government officials. Many other ethnic Albanians, in fact, were actually pressured to reject indigenous job offers in Serbian companies, in favor of joining the separatists. Open battles between Serbian and Croatian politicians manifested themselves only after a power struggle began in the Central Committee of the Yugoslav Communist party in 1989, which lasted until the Communist organization fell apart during the special 14th Party Congress in late 1990. Slovenes simply left the Congress because their demands were not met. From that moment on, the breakaway leaders worked hard on strengthening the Communist leadership of the various republics, even as they were being faced with dramatic drops in membership. Eventually the federal Communists reorganized themselves into predominantly social-democratic leftist organizations under different names.

CROATIAN ELECTIONS

At the end of 1989, and the beginning of 1990, Croatia transformed itself almost overnight into a multi-party republic and then adopted a new constitution. The fight for power was mainly between the Communists who were calling themselves the Party of Social Changes, and the former leaders of Maspok, who thought the time had arrived to prove their legitimacy. From the right side of the political spectrum, the dark-horse Croatian Democratic Union, led by a former Tito general turned historian, Franjo Tudjman, offered Croats an openly nationalistic platform. Maspok supported moderate nationalistic goals, but not the disintegration of the country, and the Communists were equally as ambiguous.

Tudjman's party refused to join a coalition with the Communists or Maspok, as he was advised to do by many domestic and foreign experts, and the elections in the spring of 1990, vindicated that decision. The CDU won about 60 percent of the parliamentary seats, although less than half of the voters cast ballots for them. The discrepancy was attributed to the political gerrymandering that the Communists had instituted when they were still in power, but provided no help this time.

There were several reasons for Tudjman's convincing victory. The Croatian Democratic Union was well organized and had financial support from a significant number of Croats living abroad. As in Serbia, national symbols were finally allowed to be displayed, which the CDU used at political meetings to help attract by far the largest crowds. The nationalists provided the clearest and most explicit platform, blaming the Communists for economic problems and promising a radical turnaround. The relatively strong former Communists had a dramatically poor political program and little experience in political fighting under democratic conditions. By advocating nationalistic causes, the Communists actually helped Tudjman come to power.

The political battle preceding the election turned into an embarrassing defeat for Croatia's most prominent personalities -- intellectuals, writers, physicians and journalists -- who ran as former Communists and lost to totally anonymous CDU candidates -- salesmen, artisans and those of similar professions. In a fight between the two extremes, Maspok appeared not to have a united political front, and was defeated handily. Its leaders, a combination of former Communists and former dissidents, were indecisive at a time when impressive political rhetoric was more important than realistic and serious political programs.

Finally, Serbs in Croatia, who made up about 12% of the population, were divided between the Serbian Democratic Party, which was only several weeks old, and the Communist party, which received only 20.8 percent of the seats in parliament. Since there was not enough time for the SDU to be registered, Serbs voted for the Communists, believing that, as the least nationalistically oriented party, they would be able to protect Serbian interests. Such hopes, however, proved to be overly optimistic.

The new multi-party Assembly of Croatia approved Tudjman as its president at its first meeting on May 30, 1990. The new Croatian government did a lot to change the appearance of the former regime, including removal of the red star from the Croatian flag. The erection of new monuments and a change of the Croatian coat-of-arms contributed to the rising tension between Croats and Serbs in Croatia, who still vividly remembered the same symbols being used by the Ustashi during World War II.

Tudjman, however, was a methodical orator, with his ultimate goal always in mind. When he was jailed in the early 1980s for his nationalist positions, he was apparently taken on a tour of the Stara Gradiska prison in Croatia, where some of Yugoslavia's more famous Communists had served time, and whose cells were now enshrined. Tudjman's response was that his cell, too, would some day be a monument. A general in Tito's army and then a historian, he sparked even more controversy by repeatedly claiming that the number of Jews, Gypsies and Serbs killed by German collaborators in the Jasenovac concentration camp in Croatia was as few as 30,000, when common consensus had previously put the number around 700,000.

Despite offending many segments of his constituency, and even upsetting his supporters by raising his own salary as president as soon as he took office, Tudjman had the ability to strike the right notes with the right people. For a long time those people were the wealthy Croats living abroad who, in return for their support, were demanding that Tudjman push even harder for Croatian independence. In addition to placating the extremists, Tudjman also had to contend with charges of racism and anti-Semitism, which he continued to bring on by making negative comments about his Serbian son-in-law and by expressing satisfaction that his wife was not Jewish, Serbian or another nationality. The indication that Tudjman persists in his political course was reaffirmed during the recent premiere in Zagreb of Stephen Spielberg's movie "Schindler's List". When asked by journalists to comment on the movie, and the Nazi genocide in it, Tudjman remained silent.

The new Croatian government also re-established Croatia's official coat of arms, that was used by the Ustashi, and reintroduced terms in official state and political documents that strongly resembled ones used by the Ustashi. Careless statements by Tudjman implying that the World War II Croatian puppet state was an expression of the historic aspirations of the Croatian people only contributed to the increased inter-ethnic distrust between Serbs and Croats. In addition to objecting to their legal and political rights in Croatia, Serbs wanted a Croatian leader to visit Jasenovac to honor all its victims in a gesture similar to that of Chancellor Willie Brandt, who visited Auschwitz in 1970.

Tudjman, however, had no desire to accommodate Serbian interests. Serbs were fired from posts in the local government, universities, mass media and the police forces. The largest and most rebellious concentrations of Serbs in Croatia were in the regions of Krajina and Slavonia. For them, the final blow was the decision by the Croatian government in the late 1980s to change the name of its official "Croatian or Serbian language" to "literary Croatian." The Serbian population in Croatia tried unsuccessfully to reverse that decision through Croatian political channels and pressure from Serbian media. Tension on both sides reached a boiling point when Croats killed Serbian policemen in Croatia and started establishing paramilitary units. Serbian irregulars in Krajina and Slavonia waged their own war of independence in the spring of 1992. After several months of inconclusive fighting and no international recognition for the self-proclaimed independent Serbian regions, the warring sides signed an agreement to put both regions under the protection of United Nations peacekeeping forces.

ELECTIONS AND DEMONSTRATIONS IN SERBIA

MILOSEVIC'S RISE TO POWER

In the late 1980s, Kosovo was rocked by renewed separatist violence and protests. The ensuing political crisis brought into conflict two former allies, close associates and personal friends: Slobodan Milosevic, chief of the Serbian Communist Party, and more restrained Ivan Stambolic, president of the Serbian Republic. The power struggle between the two was unexpected, stormy and played out according to Communist tradition. Milosevic's victory was supported by a majority of the Central Committee, the grassroots members of the Serbian party, and ultimately by a great majority of the Serbian people. Milosevic's support was founded on his opposition to the treatment of the Serbian minority in Kosovo.

The Albanian persecution of Serbs, which included humiliating and deviant forms of public abuse, awoke in Serbs a reminder of the centuries they spent under Turkish occupation. As a form of reprisal, the Turks customarily tortured and impaled people before executing them. With such memories in the minds of many Serbs, Milosevic's Socialist Party of Serbia received plenty of support when it began declaring its views with an openness unheard of under Tito: namely, that Serbs must guarantee the security of fellow Serbs in Kosovo.

In a relatively short political career that began after years of being a Communist technocrat, Milosevic provoked more reaction and passion all across the spectrum than many of Yugoslavia's career politicians. His entrance to the political arena in 1984, as the Communist party leader in Belgrade and his resulting efforts to protect Kosovo's Serbs caused conflict with Albanian leaders in Kosovo, but won the hearts of a great majority of Serbs across the country.

At the zenith of his popularity in 1988-89, Milosevic could spontaneously gather over a million people to hear him speak. But his failure was his inability to allow more meaningful democratization in Serbia. Although at the time he was the undisputed leader of all Serbs regardless of ideology, he was unable to break from Communist habits and attitudes, which distanced him from a lot of his followers. He did take steps to return to the peasants a good portion of the land confiscated in 1953, but one of his greatest political mistakes was holding allegedly free elections at the end of 1989, that were open to mostly Communist candidates. From there, democratic reform in Serbia began to regress, just as it was picking up steam in Slovenia and Croatia. Milosevic's attempts to convey the image of moving away from the country's Communist past were further damaged when his wife, Mirjana Markovic, joined a renewed Communist party whose members included several army generals. This fueled speculation that Milosevic was securing his ties to the military in preparation for a seizure of power over the entire country. He did nothing to quell these rumors when, in March 1991, police in Belgrade beat fellow Serbs who were peacefully demonstrating against his policies.

But for the most part, Milosevic returned to Serbs their self-respect and self-consciousness that could not be expressed under communism. Under Tito, residents of Belgrade, Nis and Sabac, who increasingly felt that only their national identity was indiscriminately being associated with the taboo of nationalism, found themselves needing to adopt the nebulous and equally frowned-upon identity of being a "Yugoslav." In the eyes of some Serbs, Milosevic is the one who ultimately pronounced Titoism dead and opened the door to Serbian nationalism.

The growth of Milosevic-led Serbian nationalism began by showing itself with visual symbols. Nationalist symbols included traditional coats of arms and soldier's caps, which for a long time could be worn only by peasants and not people living in the cities. But under Milosevic, Serbs were once again allowed to celebrate their traditional family holiday of Slava, which was punishable under communism by being fired from one's job. More than anything else, though, it was increased tolerance between the church and State that provided the opportunity for Serbian nationalism to emerge. Even before Milosevic came to power, relations between the Serbian Orthodox Church and the Serbian government were being reconciled, allowing for large religious gatherings and celebrations of religious holidays. Milosevic, however, advocated returning to all religious denominations property previously confiscated, but later rescinded on this issue. The press also intensified coverage of church activities. In an attempt to demonstrate renewed cooperation, the church and the Serbian government jointly organized in 1989, the commemoration of the 600th anniversary of the Battle of Kosovo, which drew about two million Serbs from home and abroad.

MULTI-PARTY ELECTIONS

In December 1990, Slobodan Milosevic was elected president of Serbia, with 65 percent of the vote. His Socialist Party of Serbia won 194 out of 250 parliamentary seats. In a presidential race that consisted of 32 other candidates, Milosevic's closest opponent, the leader of the nationalist, Serbian Movement of Renewal, Vuk Draskovic, received about 16 percent of the vote.

The victory by Milosevic and his Socialists was not a surprise, but no one thought it would be such a convincing victory. Foreign observers on hand for the voting reported no significant irregularities, but opposition candidates as well as some foreign governments raised the question of the Socialists' misuse of the mass media and premeditated pressure on voters in the interior regions of the republic. For the most part, however, Milosevic's pressure came in the form of a pledge to maintain all the securities that Serbs had been afforded under communism. These included political stability, jobs, social security, medical care and pensions. Milosevic also preached the need for Serbian unity in order to protect Serbian minority communities in the other republics. He took a strong stand in favor of the Serbian population in the mostly Albanian-populated province of Kosovo. He let it be known that the Socialists would not give up the territory, and that Serbian people, property and churches would receive protection from his government. In other words, Serbs did not vote only for Milosevic, whose authoritarian style and lack of support for democratic changes actually gave him a lower popularity rating in 1990 than in previous years. The Socialists were successful simply because they came out against uncertainty and insecurity, something the fledgling opposition movements could not guarantee.

Serbia's move toward democratization from the outset favored the Socialists and their entrenched network of grass roots organizations of the former Communist party. Former Communist activists overnight changed their party, but retained influence over the voters, including workers who were told that privatization of the economy might put their jobs in jeopardy. In addition to their own influence, the Serbian leadership was also able to capitalize on the favorable but short-lived economic spurt created by the policies of the federal government's Reformist party. The Reformists themselves were unable to shake the unorthodox stigma of being a party created by the government, instead of being created in hopes of governing. This aberration was further crystallized for Serbians when the Reformists did not compete in the Slovenian and Croatian elections being held during the same period. This all provided the Socialists with enough ammunition to convince voters that sudden leaps and experiments could be detrimental.

VIOLENT DEMONSTRATIONS IN BELGRADE
AND CHALLENGES TO MILOSEVIC

The unexpected overwhelming electoral victory by the Socialist party of Serbia prompted fears that it would not overcome its inherent Communist mentality. The people's mandate was considered a delivery of absolute power to the Socialists, while within the party, hard-liners prevailed over the advocates of more liberal policies. The result was that after the elections, Serbia was arguably less democratic than before the vote. Once in power, the Socialists resisted continuing reform efforts aimed at establishing a market economy or cooperating with opposition movements, at least in the most salient areas of national, state, and economic affairs. In other words, the ruling party disregarded the nascent multi-party system, operating just as it did under one-party rule, shunning opponents and criticism. Despite the opposition's lack of power in parliament and society in general, the Socialists' approach to governing turned out to be completely erroneous, short-sighted politics.

One glaring example of the victorious party's inclination to undermine the legality of the multi-party system was the Socialists' persistence in retaining control of the state-owned Belgrade television and radio. The director of Radio-television Belgrade at the time of the election was Dusan Mitevic, a journalist who gained notoriety in 1981, by minimizing the importance of ethnic-Albanian demonstrations in Kosovo on orders from the then-Communist government. After being rewarded for his obedience with his appointment as director, pro-government bias continued on Belgrade television not only during the election campaign, but afterward as well, mainly in the form of limited and biased coverage of opposition parties. In the election fever of its campaign coverage, Belgrade television disguised the severity of the Serbian economy, which was on the brink of collapse and probably in worse condition than the feeble economies of Slovenia and Croatia. This facilitated the implementation of a government decision to raise taxes, instead of attracting foreign capital and creating favorable conditions for small businesses. Eventually, such guided reporting drew the ire of not only many honest journalists, but also of some of the more sober, reform-minded members of the Socialist party.

Another political mistake made by the Socialists was the creation of an alliance with, or at least open affinity for, the military-dominated League of Communists-Movement for Yugoslavia, which included Milosevic's wife. The Serbian public was not willing to accept a president and first lady of the republic in different parties, and this reinforced the belief that hard-line Communists were still hiding behind the ruling Socialists.

Feeling stifled by the government and the media it controlled, the opposition chose to turn to its source of support, where it won most of its votes -- the streets of Belgrade. As was usually the case, the reason for the demonstrations was secondary; in this case it was accusations against Draskovic. In response, Draskovic called a rally in Belgrade's Square of the Republic, but local authorities refused to issue a permit for a demonstration there, saying that the masses would disrupt normal city operations. Instead the organizers were directed to a square away from the city center, across the Sava River, where the Socialists held political meetings.

Leading up to the planned demonstrations, a coalition of Draskovic's supporters offered to negotiate with the government. They promised to give up their protests if the management of Belgrade television submitted its resignation. The government dismissed the offer as an opposition threat to use the television management to discredit elected officials. As a result, on March 9, 1991, demonstrators began protesting in the Square of the Republic. The ensuing clashes with police left two people dead. Each side provided its own account of who was to blame for instigating the violence, and the findings of a joint commission, which was later disputed, placed blame on both sides. Belgrade television ignored the events, but a small independent television station, known as Studio B, was temporarily closed by authorities because it was broadcasting from the scene of the demonstrations. Studio B was accused by the government of inviting people to protest, but others said it was Belgrade television's silence that brought people out.

While the violence ebbed and flowed, the government left its mark on the people not in the number of casualties that resulted, but in the fact that for the first time in post-war Belgrade, tanks were called onto the streets. They only came out for a short time and withdrew without incident, but their actual presence caused great political damage for the socialists and the army. The worldwide coverage of this event brings to one's mind incidents in Pristina in 1968, and again in 1981, when tanks rolled through that city, but the West remained silent about the communists actions.

Expression of the opposition's anger manifested itself in mass protests led primarily by students and intellectuals. They protested peacefully, most often in the nearby Terazije Square -- without any fear that the authorities would respond with force. Not supporting any political party, the opposition showed a strong determination to have their demands met. They wanted the release of all jailed demonstrators, including the major opposition leader, Mr. Draskovic. They also continued their call for the resignation of the management of Belgrade television, as well as Interior Minister Radmilo Bogdanovic, who was considered to be responsible for misuse of the police force. Ultimately, an agreement was reached that all political action, including the investigation of the responsibility for the violence, would be conducted by legal means, and most of the opposition demands were met.

As in many of the other states that were forced to overhaul their political systems after four decades of Communist rule, the difficulties brought on by such a challenge were enhanced by two human factors. A good part of the Serbian socialist party was interested in as slow a transition as possible, in order to retain as much power as they could for the longest period of time. But there were also many socialists, well educated in Communist ways of thinking, who had difficulty comprehending the benefits of multi-party politics. Aside from political education, however, when compared to the relatively well-accepted election results in the other former Yugoslav republics, the demonstrations following the Serbian elections suggest specific incongruous difficulties in Serbia that were not visible in the other republics. The March 9th Belgrade demonstrations showed Draskovic's political inexperience or his aversion toward confrontation for backing down at the peak of his triumph, and Milosevic's sense for survival and perhaps sound political instincts by making minimal concessions in order to stay in control of the situation. Although the Belgrade demonstrations did not unseat Milosevic, the second opportunity presented itself when a Serbian-born American businessman, Milan Panic, became prime minister of Yugoslavia. Expressing a different political concept, Panic challenged Milosevic in the December 1992 elections for Serbian president. Although Serbs saw Panic as a bridge to the West and liked his American-style campaigning, Panic lost because of the lack of support of the international community. By winning more than 56% of the vote in, as some observers say, a tampered election, Milosevic remained in power in Serbia.

SLOVENIA: THE FIRST REPUBLIC TO DECLARE INDEPENDENCE

The first open inter-ethnic disagreement that directly pitted two republics against each other started in the middle of the 1970s, with the polemics between Slovenes and Serbs. One of the first more illustrative controversies erupted over a common curriculum of Yugoslav literature. Slovenia refused to include renowned non-Slovene Yugoslav writers in its curriculum, opting instead to teach lesser known Slovenian writers. About the same time, Slovenia began to emphasize its own language and required workers from other republics living there to speak only Slovenian. They also wanted all children to study in the Slovenian language.

Throughout their history, Slovenes and Serbs have had traditionally tolerant and friendly relations. In the old Yugoslav state, Slovenes often played a mercurial role in the political quarrels between Serbs and Croats, taking the side which benefited them the most. The most important post-war Slovenian politician was Edvard Kardelj, who was very influential in the writing of Yugoslavia's constitutions. Through his position, Kardelj exerted tremendous influence on the federal government and its political makeup, favoring Slovenia's economic development.

HISTORIC RELATIONS BETWEEN SERBS AND SLOVENES

Slovenes and Serbs were both able to safeguard their culture and language, under the Austrians and Italians in the first case, and the Turks and Hungarians in the latter case. But Slovenes, as a people, did not wage war, and it was a battalion of Serbian POWs returning from Austria, and armed by Slovenians, that liberated them in 1918 after the disintegration of Austro-Hungary. Serbian soldiers even maintained law and order in Slovenia during the turmoil that followed the collapse of the Habsburg Empire, because it was impossible to persuade Slovenian soldiers of the former Austro-Hungarian army to organize their own Slovenian army. Efforts by the Serbian army to fend off the rapidly approaching Italians secured for the Slovenes their borders with Italy. As a sign of recognition and appreciation, a Ljubljana street was named after the Serbian colonel who commanded the troops that secured the western borders for Slovenia.

Serbia also aided the Slovenes in 1941, when Hitler expelled tens of thousands of Slovenes from their fatherland in order to create an ethnically pure region for the Germans. In spite of Germany's occupation of Serbia, Slovenes arriving by the wagonloads were welcomed into Serbian homes until they could return to Slovenia after the war. For nearly 40 years after the war, "trains of friendship" traveled annually from Serbia to Slovenia and back, full of people who became friends during the war.

Shortly after putting their republic back together after the war, Slovenes, with the backing of federal troops, consisting mostly of Serbian soldiers, were ready to fight -- this time for the territory of Trieste. The disputed port region between Slovenia and Italy had been occupied by the Yugoslav Communist army in 1945, before being established as a free territory by the United Nations. International pressure forced Yugoslavia to back down from its claims, despite Tito's attempt to gain Soviet support for waging a new war in the name of Slovenian interests. In 1954, the Free Territory of Trieste was partitioned and control of the territory was divided between Yugoslavia and Italy.

SLOVENIA MOVES TOWARD SECESSION

While Milosevic was fostering an explosion of Serbian self-consciousness, other republics were beginning to invest in ideas to protect their own interests. Slovenia began to see itself as being hindered by other underdeveloped regions of the country that it blamed for economic hardship. Slovenes were no longer benefiting from the privileged economic status they had under Tito, and considered themselves well suited to go it alone.

According to the Constitution of 1974, the Yugoslav federal system already had many confederate aspects, such as the consensual decision-making process within the presidency, and within the presidency, Slovenia had disproportionately greater political and economic influence considering its small size. By the late 1980s, Slovenes openly opposed funding what they saw as a bottomless pit in the underdeveloped region of Kosovo. They demanded that Kosovo's leaders account for where and how over one million dollars a day in federal funds was being spent. The Albanians considered Slovenia's refusal to contribute as a lack of confidence in their ability to govern Kosovo, as well as interference in their internal affairs. Eventually, Slovenia used the Kosovo funding issue to exacerbate other dissatisfactions it had with the federal government. The industrial republic, which was advancing the process of democratization faster than the rest of the country, also enjoyed a privileged trading status with the rest of the country. Fear of losing that status within Yugoslavia played a large role in Slovenia's apprehension about remaining within the federal structure.

For several years prior to secession, Slovenia systematically cut off ties with the federal government, while at the same time seeking a dialogue without making any concessions. Slovenia's policy of peaceful secession came to a head in 1990 when Serbia decided to cut off all economic ties with Slovenia and stop importing Slovenian goods. The move was, with good reason, characterized as unfair and as blackmail by Belgrade. The economic boycott was short-lived and the circulation of goods was resumed, but the confrontation brought to the surface a trade dispute that had been brewing for years. In Slovenia, it had always been exceptionally hard to purchase industrial goods from Serbia. On the other hand, Slovenes imported from Serbia mainly raw materials and agricultural products, which they alone manufactured and profited from by reselling as final products to the rest of Yugoslavia and abroad.

Tension further heightened at the beginning of 1991 when Serbia illegally printed money through its central bank, breaking the restrictive monetary policy of the federal government, and was forced to return about 1.2 billion dollars. What angered the Serbs was an admission by the federal government that Slovenia had quietly done the same thing a few years earlier without being fined.

Other examples of preferential treatment of Slovenes included the military trial of several journalists for stealing military secrets in the late 1980s. Working with a Slovenian first sergeant, reporters from the magazine "Mladina" stole documents pertaining to federal army plans in the event of secessionist unrest in Slovenia. The journalists were tried and convicted before a military court, but the trial evolved into a fight over the Yugoslav military's right to use Serbo-Croatian as its official language. Later, Slovenian authorities allowed the convicted journalists, who did not deny their guilt, to serve their sentences under house arrest.

SLOVENIAN INDEPENDENCE

The most advanced and Western-oriented of the six republics, and favorite of the federal regime, Slovenia had the highest standard of living. Its Western style of organization, self-discipline and productivity, however, never allowed it to reach the advanced economic levels of Austria or Italy. Geographically closest to the West, Slovenes reaped their greatest benefits from illegally retained federal funds from local border traffic and from watching Austrian and Italian television programs, as well as the ability to travel short distances to get a taste of Western living. Slovenes did not show nearly as much interest in the way other Yugoslavs lived, the rights they had, or their economic plight.

As the industrial and export center, Slovenia was considered the engine of the Yugoslav economic machine, while other republics provided raw materials and the work force. In return, Slovenes had to set aside proportionally higher funds for the federal government and the Kosovo province. Slovenian Communists showed the greatest understanding and realism for the changes that were unfolding around them in the rest of Eastern Europe, but any such progressive ideas for Yugoslavia met a dismal fate at the hands of the federal Communist leadership still in power.

As in similar circumstances regarding ideology, the Slovenian government was more flexible and ready to accept reform. But it was stuck with a federal government that rightly argued that what was good for developed Slovenia was not necessarily good for underdeveloped Macedonia or Kosovo. The Slovenian solution was to stop supporting policies for the underdeveloped regions, thereby withdrawing support for the entire federal structure.

Despite losing the presidency to the Communists, the main political force in the republic was formed by the party Demos, an alliance of the Social-Democrats, the Christian-Democrats, the Peasants, the Greens and other smaller parties. The head of the Slovenian Communist party, Milan Kucan, was elected president in April 1990, by a slight majority of about 58 percent, after he "froze" his party membership. His most serious competitor, Demos candidate Joze Pucnik, was defeated allegedly because his spouse was not Slovenian-born.

The issue of Mrs. Pucnik's nationality did not stand alone in revealing elements of Slovenian xenophobia. Slovenian authorities passed a law in the mid-1980s, prohibiting Albanians from buying real estate in Slovenia.

By the end of 1990, Kucan decided his government's positions, and not how others reacted to them, should be the basis of his power. And Slovenes agreed with him. In December 1990, Slovenia became the first Yugoslav republic to pass a referendum declaring independence. As an author of the referendum, Kucan sought a gradual secession from Yugoslavia and was able to retain his popularity by advocating a moderate stance on Slovenian independence aspirations. Slovenes had originally found a more hospitable social climate by joining a federation of similar Slavic peoples, but they saw their interests falling victim to the larger groups of Serbs and Croats within their federal political structure.

Federal Prime Minister Ante Markovic responded quickly to the Slovenian declaration of independence by sending federal conscripts into Slovenia to demonstrate federal authority. When Slovenian forces were given information on the whereabouts of the Yugoslav army, the federal troops were ambushed and several killed. The actual attack, and the ensuing celebration of it in Slovenia as a military victory, was enough to convince the federal government and the Yugoslav army that Slovenia was on an irreversible road to independence.

Within the next few months, Slovenia had withdrawn from many federal regulations, including the constitution, and prevented its conscripts from serving in the Yugoslav army. Slovenes formed their own military units, established nondiplomatic missions in Washington and several European capitals, and made plans to establish their own currency, replacing the Yugoslav dinar. Slovenian representatives in all federal political organs, including the collective presidency and parliament, voted for proposals to change the government structure, which virtually amounted to an ultimatum.

Slovenia justified its actions by asserting the need for democracy, a desire to enter the European fold, and a lack of toleration with communism, which Slovenes believed was still thriving in Serbia and the federal government. They also did not want to burden themselves with what they saw as distant problems, such as Kosovo. This was not the first time Slovenia had made such political moves. Slovenia had stepped out ahead on issues such as freedom of the press, the introduction of a multi-party systemand a more favorable climate for small business. At first these moves were treated by the other republics with disgust and criticism, only to be accepted later as normal throughout the country.

MACEDONIA AND MONTENEGRO: DIRECTIONS TAKEN BY THE SMALLEST REPUBLICS

MACEDONIA

The federal Reformist Party recorded its only real success in the underdeveloped, agrarian republic of Macedonia. In their 1991 elections, Macedonians chose among the Reformists, the Communists, and an extreme nationalist party called the Internal Macedonian Revolutionary Organization, known by the acronym VMRO. The vote, however, boiled down to a race among three personalities. The Macedonian leader of the Reformists, Stojan Andov, was elected as head of the government and, Kiro Gligorov, a former Communist who was considered a reform-minded economist, was elected president. Nationalist leader Ljupco Georgijevski came up short in his bid to win a share of power.

Moves toward the creation of an independent Macedonia met with more international resistance than the efforts of any of the other republics. With a population consisting of about 20 to 40 percent ethnic Albanians, and territorial disputes with neighboring Greece and Bulgaria, Macedonia was alienated by the international community, most notably Greece's allies in the European Community. The only Greek objection to an independent Macedonia was the name of the country. Greece considered Macedonia's attempt to be recognized by that name as a claim to the territory of the same name in northern Greece -- a charge Macedonia denied. The Macedonian Church was also unsuccessful at gaining the recognition it sought from the Serbian Orthodox Church and other orthodox churches, including the Ecumenical Patriarchate in Istanbul.

Like their brethren in Kosovo, ethnic Albanians in Western Macedonia insisted on the right to be taught in their native language. They also asked that Macedonian television set aside an Albanian language channel and that parliament resolve such issues as national, cultural and linguistic rights by means of a referendum. This last request stemmed from an Albanian-community belief that they are underrepresented in parliament, with 19 out of 120 seats.

Macedonia's relatively developed agricultural sector did not make up for its energy shortage, poorly developed industry, and little or no mineral reserves. In addition to a lack of general economic development, industrialization, and natural resources, Macedonia also carried a relatively high debt incurred by so-called "white elephants," huge unproductive companies that were vestiges of the Communist period. Along with cultural schisms, such as the one within the Orthodox Church, such economic hardships provided little hope for a successful independent state. In spite of this, Macedonia proclaimed its independence in November 1991, which caused a dispute with Greece over Macedonia's name. Macedonia was nevertheless admitted to the United Nations in April 1993, with the temporary name "Former Yugoslav Republic of Macedonia" and was soon afterwards recognized by the United States and Russia.

MONTENEGRO

Montenegro was the last Yugoslav republic to formally renounce the Communist party. Only in Montenegro did Communists participate in -- and win -- multi-party elections under their old name. The reasons for such an outcome were manifold, ranging from an entrenched Montenegrin belief in its leaders to the fact that only a year or two before the 1991 elections, turmoil within the ranks of the Montenegrin Communists resulted in a purge of practically the entire older generation of its leaders.

A traditionally sparse, mostly mountaineering people, Montenegrins suffered greatly under communism for their steadfast convictions. A large number of Montenegrins were jailed during Yugoslavia's break with Stalinism in the late 1940s, mainly because they could not understand what appeared to be a spontaneous change in conviction by Tito. Montenegrins considered themselves to have a different value system from the federal leadership, and as fellow Slavs they were also connected by centuries-old emotional ties to the Russians.

But Montenegrins also had an affinity with the Slavs who make up the Serbian state that dates back to the battle of Kosovo in 1389. As essentially the same people looking for a common state, Serbia and Montenegro established a state, that evolved into Yugoslavia. They renounced their dynasty, and their king, Nicholas Petrovic, abdicated. Likewise, Montenegro held to its affinity with the Serbs as the only former republic to join the new federation of Yugoslavia in 1992. The practical basis for maintaining ties between the two states was economic support for Montenegro and access to the Adriatic Sea for Serbia.

KOSOVO: INTERNATIONAL

FLASHPOINT

SERBS IN KOSOVO

Serbs settled in Kosovo in the seventh century, but the area was under Byzantine rule until the eleventh century. Serbian king Stevan Nemanja defeated Byzantium and established Serbian rule, which lasted until the Kosovo battle in 1389. The three centuries of Serbian rule are considered the golden period of the Serbian medieval state. The most holy Serbian churches and monasteries (the Pec Patriarchate, monastery Decani and Gracanica) are located in Kosovo. During the dynasty of Nemanjics (1170-1371), Czar Dushan moved the capital of Serbia from Prizren in Kosovo to Skoplje in Macedonia, although Kosovo remained the economic and cultural center.

Serbia suffered a strategic defeat in the battle of Kosovo, the greatest battle to date between the Christian world and advancing Moslems. The losses on both sides were very heavy and the Notre Dame church in Paris reportedly rang its bells prematurely in honor of a Christian victory. Serbians, however, were unable to recover from the casualties, and eventually were subjected to Turkish rule for the next four centuries. Since the battle had the character of a religious war, Serbs considered themselves fighters in the battle for the defense of a Christian Europe and deserving of a "heavenly kingdom."

For centuries afterwards, Kosovo was the scene of continuous bloody battles, especially between 1683 and 1699, when Serbs assisted the Austro-Hungarian army in fighting the Turks.

When the Austrians withdrew, hundreds of thousands of Serbs were killed or migrated west to the areas of Lika, Krajina and Dalmatia, which were under Austrian rule and are now part of Croatia. Serbs were mainly engaged as defenders of the Christian west from Turkish attacks. In spite of the persecutions, plunders and killings, Orthodox Serbs preserved all of their holy places and objects in Kosovo and considered the region as important as Jerusalem is to the Jews and Mecca to the Moslems.

ALBANIANS IN KOSOVO

Historically, ethnic Albanians in Kosovo were rarely loyal to Yugoslav governments. They almost always collaborated with the occupiers of Kosovo; first with the Turks, from whom they accepted Islam, and then with the Austrians, Italians and Germans. This hindered Serbia's medieval state and Slavic, Christian culture. About 80 percent of the Albanians in Kosovo are Moslem, while the rest are Orthodox and some Catholics.

Albanians trace their origin to the Illyrian tribes, which became assimilated during the Roman Empire, and to the Dacans and other Indo-European peoples. Originally, they mainly raised cattle and concentrated in what is now Albania. They fought against the Ottoman Empire on several occasions, occasionally alongside the Serbs. Unlike the Serbs, they overwhelmingly accepted Islam, thereby becoming Turkish allies. The Turks started settling Albanians in the regions Serbs left, a process that continued with more or less intensity for centuries. More recently, because of perilous living conditions in Albania, Albanians have been escaping to settle in Kosovo, despite reports of human rights abuses among ethnic Albanians already there.

In 1945, the new Communist government established Yugoslavia as a federation with the autonomous provinces of Vojvodina and Kosovo, within the republic of Serbia. The borders within

Yugoslavia were determined administratively by an agreement among the top Communist leaders, without taking into consideration historic or demographic factors and traditions. Tito granted Kosovo autonomy in an attempt to further his plans for a greater Balkan Communist federation. He wanted to create a federation that would have included Albania and eventually Bulgaria, and Kosovo was intended as bait for the Albanians to agree to join. But Tito's plans collapsed in 1948, when he broke off ties with Stalin. Until the mid-1950s, Albanian strongman Enver Hodza remained part of the Communist coalition with Moscow, known as the Cominform, which alienated Tito.

Following the formation of the new federation, Albanians in Kosovo sought to gain even more autonomy by revolting against the communists, but Tito's forces put them down. A similar revolt, with similar results, took place in 1968. Three years later though, Kosovo did receive more autonomy.

According to the official census of April 1981, Kosovo -- called Kosova by Albanians -- had a population of 1,227,424 ethnic Albanians, or 75.5 percent. Serbs and Montenegrins made up about 15 percent, with Turks and other Moslem nationalities making up the rest. The census data, however, contradict estimates by the Albanian separatist lobby that Kosovo is populated by 90 percent ethnic Albanians. In addition, more than 800,000, Albanians live and work in areas outside Kosovo. According to data from 1986, the rate of population increase in Kosovo was about 30 percent, while the death rate was about 5.5 percent. In 1921, the Albanian population in Yugoslavia constituted 3.4 percent of the total population; in 1948, that ratio had increased to 4.8 percent, and in 1971 to 7.7 percent. The ethnic-Albanian population in Yugoslavia doubled between 1921 and 1959, and again over the next 22 years. It is expected to double once again by about the year 2005, putting more pressure on the rest of Serbia and Macedonia to deal with a greater percentage of integrated Albanians.

According to federal statistics in 1987, Kosovo had 224,527 workers in the industrial sector, while the rest of the working population was mainly involved in agriculture. The area of the province is 10,887 square kilometers, of which 5,644 square kilometers is cultivated land. Because of the rapid population growth, the unemployment rate was always high, which added to the dissatisfaction among ethnic Albanians, despite federal subsidies that amounted to more than one million dollars a day between 1981 and 1985.

Unemployment in the region was further exacerbated in 1989, when about 40,000 Albanian workers, teachers and officials were fired after walking off their jobs to protest Serbian rule. Teachers were objecting to a mandatory curriculum being forced upon them that was being used throughout Serbia. In general, the striking Albanians, supported financially by emigrant Albanians, were trying to worsen an already weak economy to show that Serbian rule over the region was not politically or economically viable.

During the 1987-88 school year, Kosovo had a total of 347,907 enrolled students, of which 38,951 attended the university in Pristina. Kosovo had the fourth largest growth rate of its university population for the period from 1980 to 1988 (behind the United States, Canada, and the Netherlands).

Since its founding in 1969, the University of Pristina has grown to include seven colleges, and has graduated 50,000 students. As at all levels of education in Kosovo, classes were taught in Albanian, but Turkish and Serbian and Croatian languages are used to accommodate the other ethnic groups.

ETHNIC AND POLITICAL DIVISION

In addition to being a statistically under-represented minority in Kosovo, Serbs and other non-Albanian nationalities were also subjected to persecution as well. Children were a particularly effective weapon in the ethnic battles of Kosovo. In 1989, the Serbian government decided to segregate the mixed Albanian and Serbian schools because of harassment and attacks against the Serbian children by their Albanian peers. During the 1980s, about 50,000 Serbs and Montenegrins left their homes and emigrated from Kosovo.

A series of student-led demonstrations in Kosovo in 1981, did not bring about any of the further changes that secessionist-minded Albanians had in mind, but demonstrations that continued on and off between 1987 and 1989 precipitated Kosovo's reduction of autonomy under the 1990 Serbian constitution. Kosovo's autonomy had been exercised by its own parliament and presidency, which was made up mostly of ethnic Albanians. But on July 2, 1990, the self-proclaimed parliament declared Kosovo an independent republic, and shortly afterward Serbia responded by suspending the province's government and imposing direct federal rule. In addition, state funding was withdrawn from an Albanian daily newspaper published in Kosovo, and eventually Serbian authorities banned secessionist-minded* television journalists.

Serbs became afraid of Albanian secessionist forces who claimed they would use peaceful means or force to accomplish their goals. The Kosovo government reacted to its suspension by continuing to meet covertly. Secessionist political parties then boycotted Serbian parliamentary elections in December 1990, although they likely would have won the majority of votes in Kosovo, thereby strengthening their opposition in Serbia. Albanian leaders were only interested in negotiating a settlement within the federal structure.

Federal authorities prevented a large-scale immigration to Kosovo of thousands of refugees fleeing Albania in the summer of 1991. Because of the difficulties facing them in the province, Yugoslav authorities were interested in admitting only Albanians of Serbian, Montenegrin, or Macedonian origin. Under Tito, who believed that by accepting refugees and treating them well, it would show the advantages of the Yugoslav system over the Albanian Stalinist regime, tens of thousands of Albanians immigrated to Kosovo.   But now that tension was building between the Albanians and Serbs, the federal government had no interest in continuing Tito's policy.

By 1991, Kosovo had gone from being Tito's bait to the Albanians to join a greater Yugoslavia, to being an Albanian justification for creating a greater Albania. Democratic processes in Albania had strengthened contacts between Albanians in their homeland and those in Kosovo, who were not hiding their desire to unite in one common state.   As in many regions of the world freed from decades of authoritarian rule, forces advocating democracy ran headlong into those demanding renewed nationalist identity, long suppressed by centralized governments.   In Kosovo and other areas, such as many parts of the former Soviet Union, nationalist claims by different peoples have collided with each other -- often violently -- on lands where Communist rulers imposed artificial borders to diffuse ethnic allegiances.

Slobodan Milosevic and his socialist party were the first to capitalize on the regime's inability to solve the Kosovo problem. When he promised Serbs in Kosovo that local Albanian police would not beat them any more, Milosevic won the hearts of the majority of all Serbs.   That gesture was later used as a main trump card in his political fight with the ruling Communists, who thought they still had a lock on power in Serbia. Beginning with Tito, the Communists had little interest in the disputes between the ethnic Albanians and Serbs in Kosovo.   At the eighth meeting of the Central Committee of the League of Yugoslav Communists in 1988, Milosevic rose to power by combining enough Serbian nationalism with a belief that liberalization and democratization could move Serbia forward faster than the other republics, which where still controlled by entrenched Tito-era Communists.

Milosevic was uncompromising on the question of Kosovo, seeking allies among ethnic Albanians to pursue a policy of solid alliance with Serbia. He was interested in guaranteeing equal status to the Serbs and advancing the judicial system, but he found very few such allies, as separatism had taken deep roots. The strongest argument was the numerical superiority of ethnic Albanians, whose representation kept growing because of the continuous Serbian exodus. An opportunity to tabulate the strength of the ethnic-Albanian community was lost when it refused to participate in the 1991 federal census.

Milosevic responded to secessionist violence by using repression as a means of keeping law and order. He also refused any efforts to initiate deeper democratic reforms in Serbia. The Albanian separatists, however, transformed themselves from faithful allies of the Stalinist regime in Tirana to democratic reformers overnight, which provided them with sudden support in the West. Milosevic's handling of Kosovo, however, enhanced his popularity among Serbs even though the Communist regime was not taking any real steps toward democracy or a market-oriented economy.

Adding to the disintegration of the unified state, Slovenia and Croatia were ready to free Milosevic's hands in Kosovo if he would agree to Yugoslavia's becoming a confederation. As much as this suited the Serbs with links to Kosovo, it scared the large Serbian communities in Bosnia-Herzegovina and in Croatia. Serbia's unwillingness to meet these demands, however, led to stronger Slovenian and Croatian support for Kosovo. Although later overshadowed by nationalist and economic disputes between the republics, and then the outbreak of war, Kosovo remained a source of instability between Albanians and both the Serbian government and opposition movements, who found a rare point of agreement with their steadfast stand on Kosovo.

BOSNIA-HERZEGOVINA:

INTER-ETHNIC FLASHPOINT

As a blend of ethnicities made up mostly of Moslems (about 40 percent), then Serbs (about 35 percent) and Croats (about 18 percent), Bosnia-Herzegovina proved to be the most complex, and ultimately the bloodiest, secession from the former Yugoslavia. Before the war started in Bosnia-Herzegovina, Serbs were concentrated mainly in the western regions bordering Croatia, while Moslems lived in the areas nearest Serbia, but only in cities. Croats lived mainly in central Bosnia and in western Herzegovina. But so many areas of the republic were ethnically mixed to the point that there was no logical way to divide the territory into distinct ethnic communities, without the so-called "ethnic-cleansing" that resulted.

The composition of political parties in Bosnia-Herzegovina reflected the republic's ethnic division. Moslems assembled mostly around the Party of Democratic Action, and Serbs mainly voted for the Serbian Democratic Party. Croats largely joined the Croatian Democratic Union, which was in power in Croatia.

Although Bosnia-Herzegovina was for a long time a bastion of orthodox Titoism and the main supporter of a united Yugoslavia, to the surprise of many observers, the Reformist party of federal premier Ante Markovic did not do well in the republic's 1990 elections. Such a poor showing by the Reformists was the final nail in the coffin for the still hoped-for idea that democracy could save the Yugoslav nation. A weak coalition giving equal power to Moslems, Serbs and Croats was formed by Alija Izetbegovic, the leader of the victorious Moslem party, but it proved to be an unstable government, loaded with distrust, sparks of intoleranceand a string of conflicts that spread outside the republic.

Upon assuming the presidency of Bosnia-Herzegovina after the elections, Izetbegovic became the only leader in any of the Yugoslav republics not to have had any ties with the Communist party. He was twice jailed for his involvement with Islamic organizations, the first time in 1946, which led to his spending three years in prison. In 1983, he was sentenced to 14 years for writing a book on the role of Islam in society, which advocated the overthrow of non-Islamic rule and the independence of Islamic social and political institutions. But he was released after serving nearly six years.

Interested in following the paths to independence that Slovenia and Croatia had taken, Izetbegovic sought international recognition for Bosnia-Herzegovina. He naturally found the support and aid he was looking for from Islamic countries. But as the European Community found itself at the forefront of efforts to bring peace to the region, diplomatic recognition from the EC was really what Izetbegovic felt he needed. Germany had convinced France, Britain and other EC countries, despite their reluctance, that recognition of Slovenia and Croatia was necessary. Once the European Community recognized Bosnian independence, and the United States followed suit, full-fledged war ensued.

Upon embarking on international peacekeeping efforts, neither the United Nations, the European Community, nor any of their member states, had any interest in getting involved militarily in Bosnia-Herzegovina. But they did not shy away from placing blame on the Serbs, and ultimately on Milosevic for assisting and arming the Bosnian Serbs who were fighting a civil war. The Serbs were also condemned for the practice of "ethnic cleansing," the expulsion of the non-Serb population living in Serbian regions of Croatia and Bosnia-Herzegovina. But Croatia, which initiated the practice of "ethnic cleansing" against the Serbian population in that republic, was not punished by the United Nations or the international community. The initial United Nations response was to take diplomatic action against the new state of Yugoslavia. Resolutions were passed by the U.N. Security Council imposing economic sanctions and an arms embargo on Yugoslavia. Later resolutions included a prohibition on Bosnian Serb aircraft flying over Bosnia-Herzegovina.

For its part, the European Community undertook a massive negotiating role, along with the United Nations, beginning with an international conference on the Yugoslav crisis in London in August 1992. Bringing together representatives from all the warring parties, the conference was prematurely hailed as a turning point in the Balkan conflict. The conference ended with Moslems, Serbs, and Croats ostensibly agreeing to end the use of force in the republic, to halt the practice of ethnic cleansing, to close detention camps, and to recognize the borders of the former Yugoslav republics as well as the rights of ethnic minorities within them. International relief organizations were also guaranteed more access to the war-torn regions in order to provide humanitarian aid. The result was a disproportionate ratio between the amount of time invested by chief negotiators Cyrus Vance and Lord David Owen and the amount of success achieved toward ending the war in Bosnia-Herzegovina. Geneva peace negotiations held in 1992 and 1993, under the auspices of the European Community negotiator, David Owen, and the United Nations envoy, Thorwald Stoltenberg, did not produce significant results due to Moslem intransigence and ever-increasing territorial demands. While negotiations were in process, a three-sided conflict among Serbs, Moslems, and Croats continued, producing bloody massacres. The massacre at the Sarajevo market in February 1994, although most likely staged by Bosnian Moslems, was readily attributed to the Bosnian Serbs, leading to the NATO ultimatum to the Serb forces and lifting of the siege of Sarajevo. The Serbs claim that the massacre was staged by Bosnian Moslems to provoke an international military response. NATO's military intervention was prevented at the last moment, after Russia persuaded the Serbs to withdraw and so became an instant co-player in the Balkan war. This prompted speculations on the so-called "New Yalta" approach dividing Bosnia-Herzegovina into Western and Eastern spheres of influence.

Under US pressure the warring Moslems and Croats reached an agreement in Washington on March 1, 1994 creating a Moslem-Croatian federation. Serbs rejected joining the new entity, calling it an "unnatural creation." To many political observers it appeared that the Moslem-Croat alliance against the Serbs re-created conditions that caused the civil war in Bosnia, since the Serbs perceived this alliance as a means to isolate them and tilt the military balance in favor of Moslems and Croats. The Serbs, however, continuously maintained the position that reflected two major problems in resolving the Bosnian issue: the questions of division of territory, and the right to self-determination and sovereignty. The Bosnian Moslems demanded that the Serbs accept a settlement that would give them less land than they had before the civil war, despite their victories on the battlefield. The Serbs were not willing to concede the quality and the quantity of the land that the Moslems demanded. The second matter is the right of Bosnian Serbs to self-determination and sovereignty. The Serbs do not want to be part of a Bosnian state in which the Moslems would be dominant. They want to unite with fellow Serbs in other regions of former Yugoslavia.

In July of 1994, the so-called "contact group" made up of representatives from the United States, Russia, Germany, France and Britain, offered a take it or leave it peace plan for Bosnia and Herzegovina. The Bosnian Serbs rejected the proposal, suggesting that it did not grant them recognition as an independent state, did not give them enough productive territory, including a Serbian populated section of Sarajevo, and denied them access to the Adriatic Sea. While the Bosnian Serbs wanted further modifications to the plan, the Belgrade government suddenly in August of 1994, announced that Yugoslavia opposed the decision of Bosnian Serbs not to accept the peace plan. In response to that decision, Yugoslavia cut off all political and economic ties with the Bosnian Serbs. The stunning "turning point" by Milosevic became an explosive issue, threatening to divide the Serbian society and cause deep strifes among the Serbs.

SERB ETHNOGRAPHICAL CLAIMS

The Bosnian Serb leaders Dr. Radovan Karadzic, Dr. Nikola Koljevic, Dr. Biljana Plavsic, Mr. Momcilo Krajisnik and general Ratko Mladic adhere to the principle that the Serbs should be united in a common state with its own territory and jurisdiction. The Serbs maintain that international law and practice have been repeatedly and blatantly violated by various segments of the international community in the course of the present Yugoslav crisis.

The Serb ethnographical principles rest on historic and international legal claims in the former Yugoslav republic of Bosnia-Herzegovina. From the standpoint of historical developments, the Serbs in Bosnia-Herzegovina fought during the 19th century for independence from Turkish rule and from the Habsburg state from 1878 to 1918. Their first war of liberation to unite with Serbia into one state took place in 1805. From 1852 to 1862, there was an uninterrupted chain of insurrections against Turkish rule. In July 1875 there erupted another Serbian insurrection, motivated by the efforts of the Serbs in Bosnia-Herzegovina to liberate themselves, causing substantional international crisis (The Eastern Question, 1875-78). The Bosnian crisis of 1908-09 (when the Habsburg Empire annexed Bosnia-Herzegovina), likewise became an international affair, as did the July crisis of 1914, following the assassination of Archduke Franz Ferdinand in Sarajevo, which led to the outbreak of the World War I.

The international legal basis of present Serb claims in Bosnia-Herzegovina rests on the following treaties and documents.

1) The London Agreement of 1915: contained an explicit commitment by the Entente Powers to respect the "ethnic and historic rights" of the Serbs to the entire territory of Bosnia-Herzegovina, to the Adriatic coastline south of the city of Sibenik, as well as to several parts of the present-day Republic of Serbian Krajina. The receptiveness of the international community to the legitimate aspirations of the Serb nation was thus fully confirmed in the early part of this century. The London Agreement offered the Serbs a solution -- approved by the Great Powers -- which if suggested today, would probably be condemned as an attempt to create "Greater Serbia." However, the Kingdom of Serbia opted for a Yugoslav solution, in order to bring into reality the old dream of South Slav unity, in the form of a common Serb-Croat-Slovene state. Thus the Serbs gave up their statehood as well as the opportunity to define the ethnic frontiers of the entire Serbian nation.

2) The Corfu Declaration of 1917: provided the platform for the subsequent unification of the South Slavs into a single state, calling for unity of peoples, not states, because the Croats and Slovenes did not have states of their own. They lived in the framework of the Austro-Hungarian monarchy, whereas Serbia had in the modern period begun to reestablish its statehood at the beginning of the 19th century. At the Congress of Berlin in 1878, the Great Powers extended full recognition to Serbia as a full-fledged, sovereign, and independent member of the international community. It is fully implicit in the Corfu Declaration that the right of secession, should the Yugoslav union be dissolved, resided with the constituent peoples of the newly created state and not with the administrative units within it. In addition, the Corfu Declaration confirmed the Bosnian Serbs' right to a part of the Adriatic coastline.

3) The Fourteen Points of President Wilson: (1918) called for a "free and secure access to the sea" to be given to Serbia (No. 11). In its insistence on the right of nations to exercise the right to selfdetermination, this document fully corresponded to the letter and the spirit of the Corfu Declaration.

The validity of the principles embodied in this document is in no way undermined by the passage of time. It is the denial of the rights of the Serbs to exercise this internationally recognized principle that precipitated the tragic conflicts in Croatia and Bosnia-Herzegovina.

4) The Treaties of Paris (1919): -- specifically those of St. Germain, Neuilly and Trianon, established the frontiers of the Kingdom of the Serbs, Croats and Slovenes. The territories within those frontiers were treated as a joint legacy of those three constituent nations. The Yugoslav Kingdom was treated as the legal successor of the kingdoms of Serbia and Montenegro. Those two independent kingdoms provided the new state with its international legal standing and personality, under the aegis of the structure of inherited international treaties, agreements and conventions. The above treaties all consider Serbia as a state entity and, by implication, the Serb people as a whole, which provided an essential legal, political and moral backbone to the European order, assuring legitimacy to the international community today. The principles that guided the international community in its acceptance of the South Slav state into its ranks cannot be fundamentally altered -- to the Serbs' detriment -- in setting up the new set of rules that were supposed to guide the disintegration of Yugoslavia in our time.

5) The Atlantic Charter of 1941, the United Nations Charter, and the Universal Convention on the Rights of Man: The right of the Serb people in general, and the Serbs in the former Yugoslav republic of Bosnia-Herzegovina in particular, to statehood is clear not only from legally binding international treaties from seven decades ago, but this right is also enshrined in the continuing spirit and letter of all the major documents dealing with the right to self-determination of peoples, namely the Atlantic Charter of 1941, the United Nations Charter, and the Universal Convention on the Rights of Man.

Since Yugoslavia's birth as a state was accompanied by such documents, signed by all major powers, Yugoslavia's dissolution should equally be accompanied by reference to the very same documents.

NATIONALITIES OF FORMER YUGOSLAVIA

THE SERBS

The largest nationality in the former Yugoslavia, numbering over ten million, the Serbs are of Serbian-Orthodox faith and speak Serbian. They first settled in the Balkans in the sixth century. As the founder of the first Serbian state of Raska in 1168, Stefan Nemanja proved to be one of the most effective Serb leaders during a twenty eight-year reign. Nemanja was the founder of the Nemanjic dynasty, which went on to rule Serbia for the next two centuries. In 1331, Czar Stefan Dusan, the most famous of the Serbian rulers and a member of the Nemanjic dynasty, assumed the title of Emperor of Serbs, Greeks and Albanians. Dusan's empire stretched from the Danube to the Gulf of Corinth, and from the Aegean to the Adriatic Sea. After his death in 1355, and the battle of Kosovo in 1389, the Serbian state lost its independence, falling under four centuries of Turkish rule.

The first major successful Serbian uprising against the Turks was led by George Petrovic, later known as Karadjordje and founder of the Karadjordjevic Dynasty, who liberated Serbia in 1806. However, that independence was short-lived and was followed by a second uprising led by Milos Obrenovic in 1815, which finally succeeded in regaining Serbian autonomy. The descendants of the two families, Karadjordjevic and Obrenovic, ruled Serbia until 1941. The Obrenovic dynasty ended with the assassination of King Alexander Obrenovic in 1903, and the Karadjordjevics assumed the throne, ruling Serbia and Yugoslavia until the World War II in 1941.

THE CROATS

Approximately 4.7 million Croats populate the western region of the former Yugoslavia. These Roman Catholic, Croatian-speaking people descend from ancestors who settled in the present-day territory in the sixth century. The short-lived Croatian kingdom was created in 925, with Tomislav as the Croatian king. In 1102, the Croats and Magyars were united, thus forming a relationship that lasted until 1918. The eight-century-long relationship with Hungary and the Habsburg Empire established Croatia as a semi-independent region. In 1848-49, under governor Josip Jelacic, the Croats assisted the Habsburg government in suppressing the Hungarian revolution. But instead of gaining greater autonomy, the Croats were again subjected to Habsburg absolutism.

After the Hungarian revolution, the movement for South Slav unification grew largely through the activities of Croatian Bishop Strossmayer. In contrast, the head of the Party of Rights, Ante Starcevic, rejected the idea of Slavic unity and advocated an ethnic Croatian state. In 1905, Croatian and Serbian parties formed a coalition to work toward the unification of South Slavs. A committee of Croats, Serbs and Slovenes, led by the Croatian politician Ante Trumbic, signed a 1917 declaration that contained the main principles for a future South Slav state. In 1918, Croatia cut off its ties with Hungary and Austria and joined the Kingdom of the Serbs, Croats and Slovenes.

THE SLOVENES

Slovenes, who are Roman Catholics and speak Slovenian, number about 1.8 million. They settled in what is now Slovenia between the sixth and eighth centuries. Under the rule of the

Austro-Hungarian Empire, Slovenian efforts to create a South
Slav state were stimulated by the Serbian victory in the 1912
Balkan War. Unlike Serbs and Croats, Slovenes were not able to
establish their own independent state. On December 1, 1918,
Slovenes voluntarily joined the Kingdom of the Serbs, Croats and
Slovenes.

THE MONTENEGRINS

Yugoslavia's 600,000 Montenegrins are Orthodox Serbs with a
tradition of separate statehood. Montenegro was a decentralized
society with a tribal state structure as part of the Serbian
medieval empire. Montenegro became an independent state after
the battle of Kosovo in 1389. Subsequently, it was ruled by the
Crnojevic family and bishops until 1697, when succession was
limited to the Petrovic-Njegos family.   Unlike other Balkan
nations, Montenegro for centuries maintained independence from
the Ottoman Empire because of its harsh terrain and courageous
people. Petar I Petrovic, a revered warrior and diplomat who
ruled from 1782 to 1830, considerably enlarged the area of
Montenegro. His successor, Petar II Petrovic-Njegos (1830-51),
was not only a wise ruler but a great Serbian poet. The last and
longest-reigning Montenegrin sovereign, King Nicholas Petrovic,
governed for fifty eight years until 1918. Montenegro fought
many battles against the Turks on the side of Serbia in the
Balkan wars and in the World War I. In 1918 the Montenegrin
parliament voted to become a part of the Kingdom of the Serbs,
Croats and Slovenes.

THE MACEDONIANS

Two million Macedonians are of Orthodox faith and speak the
Macedonian language. The region of Macedonia was ruled in the
middle ages by Byzantium, Serbia and Bulgaria. From the 15th

to the 20th century, Macedonians were under Turkish rule. Their national identity emerged at the turn of the century. In 1893, an active national movement was instigated by the Internal Macedonian Revolutionary Organization, an organization that sought liberation from the Ottoman Empire. Uncertainty over the Macedonian territory provoked a conflict among Serbia, Bulgaria and Greece, which was eventually resolved by Macedonian partition according to the 1913 Treaty of Bucharest. Macedonia was never defined as a political entity. At the end of World War II, the part of Macedonia incorporated into Serbia in 1910, became one of six Yugoslav republics, gaining for the first time in its history territorial and national integrity. The first grammar was written and the national institutions founded after 1945 in Communist Yugoslavia.

THE BOSNIAN MOSLEMS

The 1.9 million Moslems of Bosnia-Herzegovina speak what was known as Serbo-Croatian. Bosnian Moslems were mostly Slavs who converted to Islam while part of the Ottoman Empire, which acquired Bosnia-Herzegovina in the mid-15th century. In the 13th century Bosnia was ruled by the Kotromanic dynasty, whose most recognized ruler was King Tvrtko. Upon the fall of the Serbian Empire in the 15th century, and the Turkish invasion of Bosnia, this region became a backward Turkish province. Four hundred years of Turkish rule led to the acceptance of Islam by many of Bosnia's Slavs.

Appendix II:

BRIEF HISTORY OF THE KARADJORDJEVIC DYNASTY

In 1804, a wealthy Serbian clan chief and merchant, Djordje Petrovic -- known to his followers as Karadjordje (Black George, after his dark looks) -- led the Serbs in an uprising against the Ottoman Empire which controlled the Balkans. Karadjordje established a government in Belgrade and in 1811 was confirmed as lawful ruler and the right of succession was vested in the family.

In 1813, the Turks returned to Belgrade and Karadjordje fled to Austria. His son, Prince Alexander, came back to rule Serbia in 1842, but was deposed in 1858. In 1903, the Parliament elected Prince Peter Karadjordjevic -- grandson of Black George -- to the throne. King Peter I brought democracy and leadership to Serbia. He had John Stuart Mills' essay "On Liberty" translated into Serbian.

While the Balkan Wars in 1912 and 1913, resulted in the expansion of Serbia, the annexation by Austria of Bosnia-Herzegovina enraged the Serbs in Bosnia and neighboring Serbia. Nationalist aspirations of Bosnian Serbs for independence from Austria finally led to the assassination of Austrian Archduke Franz Ferdinand in Sarajevo in 1914 and within days World War I had begun.

Prior to the end of the war in 1918, representatives of the three peoples proclaimed by mutual consent a new "Kingdom of the

Serbs, Croats and Slovenes" under the Crown of Peter I. He died three years later. King Alexander I, who had acted as Regent for his ailing father since 1914, had earned national fame as a soldier in the Balkan Wars and World War I. In 1922 he married Princess Marie of Romania. They had three sons: Crown Prince Peter, Prince Tomislav and Prince Andrej.

The new kingdom faced many threats. Neighboring states between the Serbs and the Croats increased tensions still further. By 1929, it was clear the King had no option but to impose a Royal dictatorship. However, he did so reluctantly and promised to restore democracy to the newly re-named Kingdom of Yugoslavia once unity and political stability had been achieved. In 1934, he was assassinated in Marseilles by a Macedonian terrorist working with Croatian extremists, with Hungarian and Italian support. The French Foreign Minister, Louis Barthou, also died in the attack. King Alexander's son, Crown Prince Peter, was only 11 years old at the time when he inherited the throne. His great uncle Prince Paul -- married to Princess Olga of the Hellenes -- became Prince Regent.

By 1941, all but one of Yugoslavia's neighbors were under Nazi domination or influence. Despite his pro-British sentiments, to avoid bloodshed the Prince Regent felt obliged to sign a pact with Germany and Italy. Shortly afterwards, on 27th March 1941, Prince Paul was deposed in a coup and the young King Peter ascended the throne. Within a week, Germany, Bulgaria, Romania, Hungary and Italy invaded the country and Yugoslavia was forced to surrender. King Peter II, with the Yugoslav government, made his way via Athens and Cairo to London where he joined the Yugoslav and other European governments in exile. In November of 1945, the monarchy was illegally abolished, and Yugoslavia became a Communist state.

In 1944, while living in London, King Peter II married Princess Alexandra of Hellenes, the daughter of HM King Alexander of the Hellenes. On 17th July 1945, Queen Alexandra gave birth to a son -- HRH the Crown Prince Alexander of Yugoslavia. Crown

Prince Alexander was baptized in Westminster Abbey by Patriarch Gavrilo. His godparents were King George VI and Princess Elizabeth, now HM The Queen.

Prince Alexander was educated at Le Rosey (Switzerland), Culver Military Academy (USA), Gordonstoun (Scotland, UK) and Millfield (UK).

King Peter died in 1970 in the United States. Although the Crown Prince decided not to take the title of King, he never renounced his name or the dynastic right to the throne. In 1972, he married HIH Princess Maria da Gloria of Orleans and Braganca, of the Imperial House of Brazil. They have three sons. The eldest son, Prince Peter, was born in 1980 and the twin sons Prince Philip and Prince Alexander were born in 1982. The marriage ended in 1983. In 1985, the Crown Prince married Katherine Batis in the Serbian Orthodox Church in London. The Crown Prince and his family currently reside in London.

ADDITIONAL READING

Allcock, John B., et. al., editors. *Yugoslavia in Transition: Choices and Constraints. Essays in Honour of Fred Singleton.* Oxford; New York: Berg; New York: St. Martin's Press, 1991.

Beloff, Nora. *Tito's Flawed Legacy: Yugoslavia & the West Since 1939.* Boulder, CO: Westview Press, 1985.

Clapham, Christopher. *Third World Politics.* Madison, WI: The University of Wisconsin Press, 1985.

Cohen, Lenard. *Broken Bonds-The Disintegration of Yugoslavia.* Boulder. Westview Press. 1993

Cviic, Christopher. *Remaking the Balkans.* New York. The Royal Institute of International Affairs. Council on Foreign Relations Press. 1991

Deakin, F. W. D. *The Embattled Mountain.* London: Oxford University Press, 1971.

Denitch, Bogdan Denis. *The Legitimation of a Revolution: The Yugoslav Case.* New Haven: Yale University Press, 1976.

Djilas, Aleksa. *The Contested Country: Yugoslav Unity and Communist Revolution,* 1919-1953. Cambridge, MA: Harvard University Press, 1991.

Doder, Dusko. *The Yugoslavs.* New York: Vintage Books, 1979.

Dragic, Nada, editor. *Nations and Nationalities of Yugoslavia.* Beograd: Medjunarodna Politika, 1974.

Dragnich, Alex N. *Serbs and Croats -- The Struggle in Yugoslavia.* New York: Harcourt, Brace, Jovanovich, 1992.

Freedom House. *Yugoslavia: The Failure of "Democratic" Communism.* New York: Freedom House, 1987.

Glenny, Misha. *The Fall of Yugoslavia -- The Third Balkan War.* London. Penguin Book. 1992.

Gow, James. *Legitimacy and the Military: The Yugoslav Crisis.* New York: St. Martin's Press, 1992.

Hoptner, Jacob. *Yugoslavia in Crisis*, 1934-1941. New York: Columbia University Press, 1962.

Ivanovic, Vane. *LX: Memoirs of a Yugoslav*. New York: Harcourt Brace Jovanovich, 1977.

Johnson, A. Ross. *Yugoslavia in the Twilight of Tito*. Beverly Hills, CA: Sage Publications, 1974.

Kaplan, Robert. *Balkan Ghosts : a Journey Through History*. St. Martin's Press, New York. 1993.

Lydall, Harold. *Yugoslavia in Crisis*. Oxford: Clarendon Press; New York: Oxford University Press, 1989.

McFarlane, Bruce J. *Yugoslavia: Politics, Economics, and Society*. London; New York: Pinter, 1988.

Pavlowitch, Stevan K. *Yugoslavia*. London: Benn, 1971.

Ramet, Sabrina P. *Nationalism and Federalism in Yugoslavia*, 1963-1983. Bloomington: Indiana University Press, 1984.

Rusinow, Dennison I. *The Yugoslav Experiment, 1948-1974*. London: C. Hurst for the Royal Institute of International Affairs, 1977.

Singleton, Frederick Bernard. *Twentieth-Century Yugoslavia*. New York: Columbia University Press, 1976

Sherman, Arnold. *Perfidy in the Balkans - the Rape of Yugoslavia*. Athens. Psichogions Publications, 1992

Thompson, Mark. *A Paper House - Ending of Yugoslavia*. London. Vintage. 1992.

Wilson, Duncan, Sir. *Tito's Yugoslavia*. Cambridge; New York: Cambridge University Press, 1979.

Zimmerman, William. *Open Borders, Nonalignment, and the Political Evolution of Yugoslavia*. Princeton, NJ: Princeton University Press, 1987.